ABIDING IN THE VINE: UNITY
Learning, Living, and Sharing in the Abundant Life

RICHARD T. CASE

All For Jesus
Castle Rock, Colorado

ABIDING IN THE VINE: UNITY - LEARNING, LIVING, AND SHARING IN THE ABUNDANT LIFE

PUBLISHED BY ALL FOR JESUS
7615 Lemon Gulch Way
Castle Rock, CO 80108
www.afjministy.com

ISBN 978-1-7334151-4-9

Publisher's Cataloging-in-Publication data

Names:
Title:
Description: .
Identifiers: ISBN | LCCN
Subjects:

Printed in the United States of America 2020 — 1st ed

FOREWORD

I was thrilled when Rich Case invited me to write the foreword for his new book, *Abiding in the Vine*. I am a raving fan of Rich, having been part of a weekly telephone Bible study he has led for over a decade. Also, my wife, Margie, and I have benefited from going to one of the wonderful marriage retreats led by Rich and his wife, Linda. He not only knows the Bible inside and out, he wants to make it relevant for our day-to-day lives.

I have often talked with friends, colleagues, and business leaders about meaningful ways we can spend our time in our work and personal lives, as well as our walks with God. I believe the key to living an abundant life is to be intentional not only in what we want to achieve but also in how we want to achieve it. Few things happen without focus or direction, and this is especially true as we seek to build a relationship with God.

Too often as we lead our busy lives, we pursue our relationship with God only as time allows—perhaps in the car, walking in our neighborhood, or for a single hour on Sunday. But God wants a much deeper relationship with us than can be achieved in those rare moments. He wants us to experience an abundant life that happens only when we are in an abiding relationship with Him.

Abiding in the Vine is an invitation to learn both what it means to abide with God and, importantly, how to do it. Whether you are single or married, my friend Rich will show the way to fully understand and walk into both God's personal will for you and the abundant life God has prepared for each of us.

I encourage anyone wanting a deeper relationship with God to begin reading this book today!

—**Ken Blanchard**, coauthor of *The New One Minute Manager*®
and *Lead Like Jesus Revisited*

Early Praise for *Abiding in the Vine*

There may be no more beautiful or breathtaking description of the Christian life than the imagery of the Vine and the branches. Richard Case has masterfully taught these truths around the world. At last, you too, can study these life-changing truths with him in this brand new study! Over the years, God has used Richard to take people deeper in their walk with God as well as to enrich a host of marriages. With this new course, let me encourage you to carefully study this material on your own, with your spouse, or as a small group, and allow God to take your walk with Him, your relationships and marriages to brand new heights!

—**Dr. Richard Blackaby**, President of Blackaby Ministries International, co-author, *Experiencing God, Revised Edition*

Having been involved with many couples experiencing the weekend retreat, "Abiding in the Vine," we witnessed innumerable couples hearing from God—on their issues. Richard brings the "how to do this" in an easy-to-read book. God's promises—forgiveness, unity, and hearing from God are all packed into this extraordinary paperback. Are you wondering how to abide or how to hear from God on your own issues? Read the book, follow the steps—and see how your life can change.

—**Jake Beckel,** CEO, Revelation Pharma Corporation; and his wife, **Mary Beckel**, who have been married for 40 years

Richard Case has spoken Truth about "getting to unity" with your spouse under the Lord, and living a life together the way it was intended by God. I thought my wife and I had a pretty good marriage, yet living in unity with God keeps making our life together better and better. We are grateful to Richard for revealing—and, with his wife, Linda—living this truth.

—**Rich Cocchiaro**, Vice Chairman, Co Founder, Kforce, Inc., and his wife, **Janet Cocchiaro**

I have had the privilege of leading nearly one thousand people through Richard Case's *Abiding in the Vine*. When a person or couple hears from their Heavenly Father on an issue that is important to them has been life changing for them, and for me. Besides receiving Jesus, abiding with God is the most important thing a person can do. This book shows you how.

—**Edward Edward Kobel**,
President and COO of Debartolo Development

Essential to a successful, abundant life is knowing the will of our Father. Richard Case's work *Abiding in the Vine* will help you exchange frustration and uncertainty for fruitfulness and peace by demystifying the invitation of Jesus to "abide." It's *the* game changer.

—**Mike Sharrow,** CEO, The C12 Group

It is a privilege for me to share my strong endorsement of *Abiding in the Vine* from Living Waters and Rich and Linda Case. Having been through the material many times myself, both as a participant and as a facilitator, I have experienced the amazing truths of abiding. The greatest blessing is a personal, intimate, abiding relationship every moment of every day with the God of the universe who loves each of us beyond all understanding. Once one experiences hearing from God and the leading of the Spirit, there is no other way to live.

—**Dave Dunkel,** CEO, Kforce, Inc.

DEDICATION

I dedicate this book to my wonderful wife, Linda.
Over our 50 years of marriage, she has faithfully "Abided in the Vine,"
has walked in the Spirit, and has always been willing
to go to unity in the Spirit with me on all our decisions and issues of life.
Together, we have lived out God's will—best and none better:
a life of peace and joy, a life of seeing God's supernatural work,
with one adventure after another.
What a privilege and blessing this has been,
as we have together learned that *apart from Christ,*
we can do nothing, but *with Christ* we can do everything!
Our life together is and has been wonderful.

Acknowledgments

We are very grateful for our children, Peter and Shara (and their two sons, our grandsons, Joshua and Aidan), Michelle, and Christina and Mark (and their three daughters, our granddaughters, Nicole, Rachael, and Riley). We so appreciate their love and support.

We wish to acknowledge The Blackabys, Henry and Richard, who have taught us such inspiring Biblical truth and how to deepen our experience with the Living God through abiding.

We so appreciate those who have walked with us over the years spiritually and encouraged us to spend time writing down what we were teaching: Tim and Mary Beth Sotos, John Beckett, Kevin Beckett, Morrison Carter, Ken and Margie Blanchard, Tom and Barbara Crates, Dirk Davidson, and our special comrade, Dave Dunkel.

Also, there are several co-laborers in Christ who have greatly contributed to helping us process the truth of abiding and unity. These good friends and leaders are those with whom we are doing life together and are "giving it away" through our Living Waters Retreat Ministry: Jake and Mary Beckel, Joe and Leigh Bogar, Rich and Janet Cocchiaro, Larry and Sherry Collett, Dave and Melissa Dunkel, Tom and Susanne Ewing, Rick and Kelly Ferris, Joel and Christina Gunn, Scott and Terry Hitchcock, Chris and Jacklyn Hoover, Rick and Nancy Hoover, Tad and Monica Jones, Ed and Becky Kobel, Don and Rachelle Light, Morgan Lucas, Chris and Heidi May, Terry and Josephine Noetzel, Steve and Carolyn Van Ooteghem, Lynda and Preston Pitts, Dan and Kathy Rocconi, Bob and Kerri Rockwell, John and Michelle Santaferraro, Denny and Allyson Weinberg, Neal and Cathy Weisenberger.

Our heartfelt thanks for and to all.

TABLE OF CONTENTS

INTRODUCTION

Throughout my life as a believer, pastor, church planter, and author, I have found that most of my fellow believers fall into one of two categories: those who attempt to spend time in God's Word or do devotions on a regular basis, and those who would like to but think they are too busy to do so.

Abiding in the Vine: Unity is an invitation to both groups, regardless of whether you are married or single. This invitation asks you to consider the abundant life promised to those who daily abide in God's Word and who cherish the notion that a beautiful relationship with God is waiting. It is my hope that this work brings married couples and singles into a deeper relationship with God. For those who do meet with God regularly, *Abiding in the Vine: Unity* will take your learning and understanding into a far deeper level. For those who believe they are too busy, *Abiding in the Vine* will reveal the value and truth of making God a true priority. The church has taught believers how to study the Bible and learn about God in Christian principles, but rarely has it taught believers how to abide and experience the abundant life that comes through THE FRUIT of abiding. This book will demonstrate both what abiding is, and importantly, how we are to rely on the Holy Spirit to do it. As told in John 16:13-15, the Holy Spirit will act as your guide to take you into the depths of personal abiding and further unity with God.

As you begin to understand the beauty of abiding, I also will show you that it is possible to fully understand and walk into God's personal will for you through a beautiful process called *unity*. This will be especially beneficial both in your married life or with your close personal friends, if you are single.

Throughout our lives, we will be confronted with daily decisions. When we abide, God will reveal all His beautiful and wonderful plans through these decisions and will do so in a way that is fully relatable. We don't have to guess at them or wonder if we will have to wait and learn from our mistakes. He will show us His perfect will. When this perfect will is revealed to us through abiding, we will see that any mistakes or issues we currently are experiencing can be restored based on His sovereignty. We just have to be willing to abide and follow Him. This may seem difficult or intimidating, but there is no requirement for prior education or spiritual maturity—the benefits of abiding are available to everybody, with the only requirement being a desire to abide. To begin on your journey of abiding, I encourage you to work through each verse and apply it to your personal situations. Review the entire book so you can learn to abide fully. Then receive the joy and beauty of this lifestyle throughout the rest of your life. From this point forward, it will dramatically change you as you learn to experience the fullness of God in His plan for abundant life for you.

SECTION 1
ABIDING

CHAPTER ONE:
What Does it Mean to Abide?

Let the Word of the Lord dwell in you richly.—Colossians 3:16

It is often said that the first year of marriage is one of the hardest of all. Why? Because it is during this time that the couple sees the other in their truest form, as their most real self. And, because the couple is in love and has made a commitment to each other, the two invest the time necessary to begin solidifying their union. They spend time together, they learn about each other, they work through their issues and, eventually, find a love far stronger than that they expressed even on their wedding day.

But this doesn't happen unless true time and effort are put into the relationship. A dinner once a month or a quick walk around the block after church on Sundays aren't nearly enough to unite the couple in a devoted relationship, and it certainly will not bring about a unity in the spirit or in their thinking. Those come by intentionally investing time in their relationship— each and every day.

Similarly, to achieve an intimate relationship, a unity of Spirit with Jesus, follower must abide deeply and truly in this relationship, beginning in God's Word—and it must happen each and every day. To abide means to learn to know, to come to know, to get a knowledge of, to perceive, to feel, to understand, to receive the truth and wisdom that He is speaking to us. That, in turn, leads to liberty, freedom, peace, release and God's wonderful fulfillment of His plan for us—changing our circumstances as only He can do. Reading a daily devotion or starting your day with a verse-of-the-day isn't enough to achieve this. He wants far more than this and rewards us mightily when it's achieved. It takes abiding—intimate time with Him—and learning to walk with Him all the time as we are guided and led by His Spirit.

By harnessing the power of the Holy Spirit, this investment brings about a new life filled with exceptional living and special privilege that, until that time, may have felt unimaginable.

To grasp this further, consider Jesus' thoughts on the beauty and benefits brought by moving into a deeper relationship (an abiding relationship) with Him.

On the night Jesus took His disciples to the upper room, He summarized key spiritual truths in what is called the Upper Room Discourse (John 13, 14, 15, 16). Here, He spent much of this time discussing the Holy Spirit and the role He would play in the believer's life after the resurrection—to be resident with us. He explained that through the Holy Spirit, we have the special privilege of God within us—leading, guiding, communicating, speaking.

As Jesus was known to do, He used an analogy to clarify His meaning; this time it was through the analogy of a vineyard, vines, and winemaking.

In over 2,000 years, vineyards and winemaking have not changed much. Of course, things are now more sophisticated in measuring and charting in the vineyard, but the process still has yet to become mechanical or automated. Even today, winemaking is an art, and the veracity of the vineyard and winemaking still remain as they did so many years ago. Jesus used this timeless analogy to express beautiful truths about the essence of Abiding, which is the basis for the relationship He intended for us: to be in and with HIM.

In John 15:1-5, we begin to understand the depth of this analogy and how critical this is to the our daily Christian life in HIM.

> I am the true vine, and my Father is the vinedresser. [2] Every branch in me that does not bear fruit he takes away, and every branch that does bear fruit he prunes, that it may bear more fruit. [3] Already you are clean because of the word that I have spoken to you. [4] Abide in me, and I in you. As the branch cannot bear fruit by itself, unless it abides in the vine, neither can you, unless you abide in me. [5] I am the vine; you are the branches. Whoever abides in me and I in him, he it is that bears much fruit, for apart from me you can do nothing. (**John 15:1-5, ESV**)

In these verses, Jesus refers to Himself as the vine, which is the sole source and provider of our "lives"—He provides everything necessary for us to live out what He intends so that our lives can be wonderful and spectacular!

The Vinedresser is the Father. He makes all the decisions during the entire process—what grapes to grow, when to water, how much to water, when to prune, how much to prune, when to harvest, how to process into wine, etc. Not a single decision is made by anyone BUT the Vinedresser. This means He makes both, the big decisions AND the everyday decisions, because He is the one who has His plan on producing the fruit that He so desires for our lives. With that in mind, we particularly need to be aware of our role as branches—to be connected to the Vine (abide). We especially aren't trying to be the Vinedresser and make our own decisions.

Usually, though, we operate with our own plans and decisions and want God to provide blessings for these choices. However, in order to achieve this level of obedience, we are to let God act as the true Vinedresser and surrender to His decision-making—just as the branches rely on the vine. The choice is ours to abide and stay connected. As we embrace this life (as a branch), we should expect that one of the Vinedresser's activities in our lives as a branch will be to prune us, which is nothing more than cutting back. If we aren't pruned and are simply left alone, the branches get too big. When this happens, the sap gets consumed by the branch and never reaches the fruit, and thus there is no fruit. So our Vinedresser has to cut back healthy branches so that the life of the vine flows through the branch and reaches the fruit. This is a continual process since the branch is continually growing. In this analogy, the pruning refers to the activities of our lives, which are continually expanding and need "cutting back." We have to continually allow the Vinedresser to give us wisdom and insight to cut back our activities. In doing so, we can create margin and space in our lives so that we are able to allow Him to create fruit. This is a real challenge in today's busy lifestyles.

The end result God seeks is to produce fruit. Fruit, more fruit, much fruit! He does this when we abide spiritually. We cannot produce this fruit by ourselves (although, as Christians, we certainly try). Interestingly though, God by Himself will not produce fruit as a Vine or a Vinedresser—He needs us as branches to be connected to the Vine, with the Vinedresser making all the decisions to produce fruit. It's an interconnecting process. God has set it up so that we are bearing His fruit. When we choose to abide in the Vine, He chooses the fruit. No abiding means no fruit. This is why His next statement is so critical.

> [5] I am the vine; you are the branches. Whoever abides in me and I in him, he it is that bears much fruit, for apart from me you can do nothing.
> **(John 15:5, ESV)**

Jesus clearly states that apart from Him, you can do nothing.

Since He says that this abiding relationship is critical to producing fruit and that apart from Him we can do nothing, the next question that needs to be addressed is: "What must be done to learn how to abide?" In the pages that follow, we will reveal to you the kind of life that will be provided by the Vine as well as the type of fruit He will create.

When we think of abiding, we tend to think first of spending time in God's Word. Unfortunately, there are many reasons why people don't spend time in the Bible. Discovering or being aware of these obstacles is the first step in removing them.

In the past, I have discipled several executives, many of whom say they do a devotion every day. I then ask, "What did it say to you last week?" Often times, they simply can't remember. Last week, two days ago, yesterday, today? They can't remember. "Maybe it was something about love," they say. "Maybe I am supposed to be more loving?" In other words, they read it, it was interesting, they enjoyed it at the moment, but they were not abiding, not receiving it in a way that the Word was changing their lives and producing fruit. While Bible study and reading the Bible are extremely important, neither are abiding. Abiding is relationship and is a privilege we have with God, who wants and enjoys producing fruit in our lives.

I have also met with couples in various workshops and retreats. So often, in these settings, the couples discussed how regularly they share their time with God. Many mention a weekly Bible study or attending Sunday church. Some start their day with a 10-minute devotion. But these are only the beginning of what is meant by true abiding.

As we consider the thought processes noted above—all of which are valid—we also must consider the real issue: We have never experienced abiding as valuable, so have never made real time for it. If I could be invisible and follow you around for two weeks, I would find out what has become valuable to you—where you spend your time and where you spend your money. You have sorted out your life where you find things valuable; and abiding in the Word is often just not valuable because you have not learned to experience how wonderful and essential it can be. It has been difficult, disappointing, overwhelming—and certainly not valuable. Throughout this book, as you learn and experience the value of abiding, you never again will relinquish this special privilege we have and the resultant fruit we receive.

In John 8, Christ takes us to another strong statement—an if/then statement. In Scripture, when we come across this type of statement, it is conditional; in order to receive the promised result, we must meet the condition; it is not automatic.

> [28] So Jesus said to them, "When you have lifted up the Son of Man, then you will know that I am he, and that I do nothing on my own authority, but speak just as the Father taught me. [29] And he who sent me is with me. He has not left me alone, for I always do the things that are pleasing to him." [30] As he was saying these things, many believed in him.
> [31] So Jesus said to the Jews who had believed him, "If you abide in my word, you are truly my disciples, [32] and you will know the truth, and the truth will set you free." **(John 8:28-32, ESV)**
>
> [36] So if the Son sets you free, you will be free indeed. **(John 8:36, ESV)**

In light of Christ telling us that apart from Him we can do "nothing," we are called to develop a passion for abiding and a passion for pursuing truth. We are able to develop these passions because we can operate in this life as Christ operated when He lived as a human—fully dependent on hearing and doing only what the Father revealed to Him. We have this capability because we have Christ living in us through the Holy Spirit. This is why He gives us this condition—if we abide in him, we can know the truth, and it will set us free. As we develop this passion for abiding and the passion for the truth—not just intellectually knowing about the truth but experiencing the truth about all things regarding the personal circumstances of our particular lives—we will be set free.

We will have a wonderful perspective of not being burdened by the normal obstacles and difficulties of life, but always knowing that we will be led by the truth into the freedom of His grand plan and larger picture for our lives—along with an abiding trust in Him and His love for us. We also will know that when He sets us free from our burdens or from those areas that affect us negatively (pornography, addictions, etc.), that freedom will not be temporary, nor will it mean that we simply manage these burdens. Instead, we will receive true transformation.

With these two passions, we, as a branch, will be driven to enjoy being with Him, our Vinedresser. We will keep pursuing truth and will be excited to learn all that He wishes to reveal to us. We will never be afraid of the truth because we know that His will and His desires for us are for our best—all of which are based upon the condition of abiding in His Word.

SECTION 2:
GOD'S PLAN

CHAPTER TWO
What Is God's Plan for Our Lives?

God has a plan for each of us. As we learn to abide, that plan is not only revealed to us, but we begin to understand a far bigger picture of the how He intends to unfold our lives into His master plan. So, then, we need to learn what it means to us as we begin abiding and what God's original intention for our abiding was and is, especially as it relates to our marriages and other close relationships. This will help us understand the bigger story of the fruit that He wishes to provide in our lives.

God had created heaven and Earth, and man and woman, to live in this perfect place with a design and purpose intended to have us enjoy exceptional living with Him eternally. Genesis 1 and 2 offer us context to understand the characteristics of this design and purpose, and to show why abiding is now crucial.

God's original intention for His creation—including the Earth in the universe, animals, plants, and, of course, man and woman—was that we would be in a personal relationship with Him. In the Garden of Eden, prior to the fall, man and woman were given authority and provision over God's creation. His plan allowed for mutual fellowship and for a life filled with abundance. Consider Genesis 1:26-31.

> [26] Then God said, "Let us make man[a] in our image, after our likeness. And let them have dominion over the fish of the sea and over the birds of the heavens and over the livestock and over all the earth and over every creeping thing that creeps on the earth."

> [27] So God created man in his own image,
>
> in the image of God he created him;
>
> male and female he created them.
>
> [28] And God blessed them. And God said to them, "Be fruitful and multiply and fill the earth and subdue it, and have dominion over the fish of the sea and over the birds of the heavens and over every living thing that moves on the earth."[29] And God said, "Behold, I have given you every plant yielding seed that is on the face of all the earth, and every tree with seed in its fruit. You shall have them for food. [30] And to every beast of the earth and to every bird of the heavens and to everything that creeps on the earth, everything that has the breath of life, I have given every green plant for food." And it was so.[31] And God saw everything that he had made, and behold, it was very good. And there was evening and there was morning, the sixth day. **(Genesis 1:26-31, ESV)**

The "us" spoken of in verse 26 is the Trinity—Father, Son, and Holy Spirit—eternally God, three in one, all completely one God yet three distinct persons. While this may be difficult for us to comprehend, the key is that Christ, the Son, and the Holy Spirit are not created beings, but are fully God and eternal. The Trinity is ever powerful and indeed able to offer us a life of abundance once we learn to abide. This was God's hope for us as He created man and woman in His image and with His characteristics. We were given the privilege of living with intimate relationship with Him. When God looked at man and woman, He saw Himself—the image of Himself. Not God and not functioning as God (though characteristics of God), but created beings to live with God, enjoy God's creation, and to enjoy fellowship with God in body, soul, and spirit. Each of the three was used for unique purposes—all of which would help us abide more deeply. He created the body as a physical being that could operate and function in the world God created. He created the soul, or as defined in the Scripture as the heart, as a place to house our emotions, intellect, personality, and will. Our soul will last eternally and will define us when we pass into eternity (whether in heaven or hell) and will be used to recognize each other in eternity. The spirit is the nature that allows us to connect with God and have an intimate relationship with Him—since He is Spirit.

The most important thing to understand, though, is that Adam and Eve did have a spiritual element of their nature that gave them the ability to communicate with God and have intimate relationship with God, who is Spirit. In the garden of Eden, God took on physical form. The key to their relationship was not their spiritual dimension but that they were sinless and so could look directly upon God in His physical form, something even Moses could not do. While they were still sinless, though, God bestowed on them free will, as He desired a relationship that was both mutual and meaningful. This sits at the heart of abiding.

Free will is not arbitrary or something God created to cause us to fail, but rather a profound part of the image of God and deeply rooted in our relationship with Him. He created us to love Him and desires us to have the freedom to choose to love Him or reject Him, which is why abiding is a choice. He will never force us to abide, but always invites us to do so.

For example, a friend called me and said he had received an insight after he and his wife had gone through yet another "deep spat," where both ended up emotionally hurting the other. The epiphany that came to him was that he was not loving his wife as Christ so loved the church even though he was trying to in his own power for quite some time. He admitted that he was actually getting worse at it, and making things worse as he was trying. He asked for my help. I taught him how to abide, showing him that he needed to be a branch. He needed to allow the Vinedresser to bring the fruit through him abiding in the Vine as a branch. He would see that love would come as he abides in God's teaching him and giving him love. But it was a choice, an invitation. He would not force him or automatically give it to him just through a wishful prayer; he would need to abide; and that if he responded to the invitation, the fruit will be guaranteed. I assured that it would happen. The love for his wife would be given, and the relationship that was strained would change as he learned how to live out this abiding.

In verse 26, God gave man and woman authority, dominion, and power over the Earth—in other words, He transferred that authority to man and woman for them to be co-creators and have dominion over this Earth that He created.

Another wonderful element of God's exceptional life for Adam and Eve in Genesis 1 is that God gave plants, animals, and every conceivable natural material so that everything was already available for Adam and Eve to live on, to build, to create. They didn't have to provide anything themselves. God was their provider—and He provided everything! Today, that provision comes to us in the form of income (more than our expenses) and also means we can live in freedom. Even today, God still wants to be our provider. As was His original intention, He still wants us to have enough income so that we can live comfortably (which means it is His intention that He provides more than we spend so we can live comfortably and without financial stress. This does NOT mean He has promised each of us material wealth. Instead, it means financial freedom in line with His plan for us).

And, as Genesis 1:31 says, everything He had created was exceptionally good, over-the-top good, superlative, supernaturally good—fantastic.

In Chapter 2, we find even more detail of this exceptional creation that Adam and Eve were given. Chapter 2 is not sequential to Chapter 1 but does go into further detail of that which God created in Chapter 1. In Genesis 2:8-25, we see:

> [8] And the Lord God planted a garden in Eden, in the east, and there he put the man whom he had formed. [9] And out of the ground the Lord God made to spring up every tree that is pleasant to the sight and good for food. The tree of life was in the midst of the garden, and the tree of the knowledge of good and evil.
>
> [10] A river flowed out of Eden to water the garden, and there it divided and became four rivers. [11] The name of the first is the Pishon. It is the one that flowed around the whole land of Havilah, where there is gold. [12] And the gold of that land is good; bdellium and onyx stone are there. [13] The name of the second river is the Gihon. It is the one that flowed around the whole land of Cush. [14] And the name of the third river is the Tigris, which flows east of Assyria. And the fourth river is the Euphrates.

[15] The Lord God took the man and put him in the garden of Eden to work it and keep it. [16] And the Lord God commanded the man, saying, "You may surely eat of every tree of the garden, [17] but of the tree of the knowledge of good and evil you shall not eat, for in the day that you eat[a] of it you shall surely die."

[18] Then the Lord God said, "It is not good that the man should be alone; I will make him a helper fit for[b] him." [19] Now out of the ground the Lord God had formed[c] every beast of the field and every bird of the heavens and brought them to the man to see what he would call them. And whatever the man called every living creature, that was its name. [20] The man gave names to all livestock and to the birds of the heavens and to every beast of the field. But for Adam[d] there was not found a helper fit for him. [21] So the Lord God caused a deep sleep to fall upon the man, and while he slept took one of his ribs and closed up its place with flesh. [22] And the rib that the Lord God had taken from the man he made[e] into a woman and brought her to the man. [23] Then the man said,

"This at last is bone of my bones
and flesh of my flesh;
she shall be called Woman, because she was taken out of Man."[f]

[24] Therefore a man shall leave his father and his mother and hold fast to his wife, and they shall become one flesh. [25] And the man and his wife were both naked and were not ashamed. **(Genesis 2:8-25, ESV)**

Many of us have a tendency to think the Garden of Eden was a small patch in the backyard, that Adam and Eve were there for about an hour, fell to the temptation of Satan, became sinful, caused the sin nature, and were forced out. Rather, they enjoyed the perfect life of the massive place of paradise (hundreds of miles by hundreds of miles) for likely many, many months, if not years, working it, naming the animals, and having communion with God. They were very active there in this big beautiful place that was the center of the world.

They were intended to be fruitful and multiply and take this beautiful place and expand it throughout the entire rest of the world. There they were given authority as they named animals, explored, and enjoyed their lives together with God. Their lives were full and happy. They enjoyed all of this prior to the temptation offered to them at the tree of "Knowledge of Good and Evil." Remember, this was not some special tree that had different characteristics or some special fruit, rather it was one of the normal trees in the Garden that was identified by God as one not to eat (setting up the opportunity to express free will, which is part of the image of God). Prior to the fall, God's intentions for us were beautiful. He had a wonderful path set for us that would endure through the ages.

As humans, we are to live in a physical world with 24 hours (approximately 16 of which are waking, and eight of which are sleeping). We are to get up and get to work, enjoying occupation; creating, building, using our skills and gifts, and enjoying fellowship with others to make progress and advancement. Then, we are to leave work at a reasonable time (after 89 hours) and spend the rest of our waking hours enjoying our spouse, family, and friends in unity of communion. This kind of living fulfills God's purpose and mission for our lives as He directs us to be a joy and full of adventure, rest, and fun. The two are to become one. This is a principle in life—to work together toward unity, agreement, and harmony, so that a married couple or friends would discover God's will together and live in God's best for them. God asks us to seek unity through the Holy Spirit. But in doing so, He doesn't ask us to give up our own perspective and thoughts on issues and decisions for the sake of unity (thus, as we will explore further, it is okay to disagree), but instead to work together in joy to come to unity with Him together. Our lives were created with a privilege—to have occupation and enjoy each other—all within our authority and provision given by God. He offered them, and now offers us, a relationship filled with His abundance.

Living as children of the King—the Creator—is called Identity. Adam and Eve did not reject who or whose they were. They fully understood their identity as they were children of the King of the universe, the creator of all things, who had provided them this exceptional place with exceptional things—and given them the opportunity to work and to live together in unity to enjoy all that they were given. Their identity was rooted in who created them—in whose image they were created. They did not consider themselves second class or unworthy of being in God's family. Instead, they abided and enjoyed the privilege of being in God's family. If you are wondering what this might look like in modern day, consider the role Kate Middleton plays in her royal family. She married into royalty and became a member of the family. She did not reject this inclusion or think she did not deserve being part of the family, but rather fully understood her new identity and privileges of being part of royalty. She was fully included.

Adam and Eve also were blessed with good health and complete communion with God. They enjoyed talking every day with God and fully and clearly understood this communion and fellowship—it was intimate, personal, and a two-sided discussion.

Because God would never force us to be obedient or into a relationship with Him, this test in the Garden can be seen as the essence of His desire for us to have free will. Adam and Eve, as part of humanity, had to decide if what they had on their own was a better thing than what God could offer. It was never God's intention to force His will on us, but rather offer us an intimate relationship that comes through abiding.

We can now see the many characteristics that represent all that God had intended for us prior to the fall: authority, provision, work, relationships, health, identity, and, of course, communion with Him.

CHAPTER THREE
How Does Christ Remedy the Fall of Humanity?

The exceptional living given to Adam and Eve in the Garden of Eden was offered by God and was His original plan for all of mankind. Not only were the two given authority over all the Earth, but they also were asked to be fruitful and multiply so that all the Earth beyond the original Garden of Eden would provide the perfect place for mankind to experience the exceptional living (the exceptional characteristics described in Chapter Two) planned by God. However, Satan came to the Garden of Eden and tempted Adam and Eve, according to the test of the free will (using the Tree of the Knowledge of Good and Evil).

There is a lot to consider when discussing man's fall in the Garden. First, where did Satan come from? We know he was a fallen angel. Originally named Lucifer, he was an angel of light who was one of the original created angels and part of the host who enjoyed life with God in heaven. He was a leader in heaven and had great stature. But as an angel created by God, we must note that Satan is not God and does not possess the qualities of God. This is one of the myths for most believers: that Satan and God tend to be somehow equivalent in power and scope, especially in today's world. Satan is not omnipresent, omniscient, or omnipotent. Rather, he is finite and only has the characteristics and the powers of a spiritual created being.

As a leader in heaven, and also having a free will, Lucifer decided to attempt to become equal to God and achieve dominance in heaven. Of course, not being God, he had no power to achieve his overthrow bid and was cast out of heaven. Since all the angels had free will, God turned to them all to ask who they wished to follow. God or Lucifer? We know that one-third followed Satan (Revelation

12:4) and are now operating with Satan in what is called the spiritual realm as demons. Thus, two-thirds remained with God in heaven and are now operating in the spiritual realm as angels. In Revelation 5:11, it says that 10,000 x 10,000 are now worshiping God, so that number would equal 100,000,000, if taken literally. So, whether it is literal or just representing a massive number of angels, the good news is that there are twice as many angels as demons; and that an angel's purpose in our lives is to minister to us! (Hebrews 1:14) We will explore further the role of the demonic so that we can understand how it impacts this broken world and us specifically.

So now, Satan and his demons (one-third of the total original angels) had access to Earth and to Adam and Eve, but had no authority to bring destruction per se. Satan knew he had to appeal to Adam and Eve to exercise their free will and disobey God. This would give Satan authority over Adam and Eve (refer to Genesis 1:26), and alter the nature of Earth, which meant that Satan's nature of destruction would dominate the Earth if he succeeded in convincing Adam and Eve to follow him and disobey God.

Satan, then, taking the form of a serpent, appealed to Adam and Eve in the Garden of Eden to bring about this test of the free will. In Genesis 3:1-7, we read:

> Now the serpent was more crafty than any other beast of the field that the Lord God had made.
>
> He said to the woman, "Did God actually say, 'You shall not eat of any tree in the garden?'" [2] And the woman said to the serpent, "We may eat of the fruit of the trees in the garden, [3] but God said, 'You shall not eat of the fruit of the tree that is in the midst of the garden, neither shall you touch it, lest you die.'" [4] But the serpent said to the woman, "You will not surely die. [5] For God knows that when you eat of it your eyes will be opened, and you will be like God, knowing good and evil." [6] So when the woman saw that the tree was good for food, and that it was a delight to the eyes, and that the tree was to be desired to make one wise, [b] she took of its fruit and ate, and she also gave some to her husband who was with her, and he ate. [7] Then the eyes of both were opened, and they knew that they were naked. And they sewed fig leaves together and made themselves loincloths. (Genesis 3:1-7, ESV)

Satan appealed to Eve (and thus, to Adam, who was right there with her) to use her own free will to eat of the forbidden tree. He suggested that God had not forbidden them to eat of the tree, that they would NOT die, and also that doing so would make them more like God—and wasn't that appealing in their desire to reach their full potential? Clearly, the real mistake that Adam and Eve made at this point was having uncertainty and questions about what God had said and what He meant (which was understandable), BUT not going back to God, with their open and perfect communion (their wonderful privilege), and ask God again to speak on this. They just came to their own conclusions (based upon the temptation of what they heard from Satan), decided on their own what they wanted to do and ate of the forbidden tree—exercising their free will and disobeying God. At that moment, they did die, as forewarned by God. So, at the fall, the spirit of both the man and the woman died (either the Holy Spirit vacated or they lost this wonderful spiritual nature and thus, their connection to and communion with God). They became a very sophisticated, intellectually superior animal now driven by instinct and self-centeredness. Their nature changed (a sin nature devoid of the Spirit of God and no longer fully able or holy enough to have direct relationship with God because He is holy and requires perfection).

Furthermore, the nature of the world changed. It went from one filled with the beauty and all the goodness of God to one whose nature was that of Satan— steal, kill, and destroy (John 10:10); and is still under the domain (authority) of the enemy.

In 1 John 5:18-20, which takes place about sixty years after the resurrection and after Christ had established His Kingdom (A Spiritual Kingdom) on Earth, the world likewise continued to function under the kingdom of the enemy. So now there are dual kingdoms. (We will further explore how we operate in and enjoy God's Kingdom while we are living in the enemy territory of Satan's kingdom):

> [18] We know that everyone who has been born of God does not keep on sinning, but he who was born of God protects him, and the evil one does not touch him. [19] We know that we are from God, and the whole world lies in the power of the evil one.

> [20] And we know that the Son of God has come and has given us understanding, so that we may know him who is true; and we are in him who is true, in his Son Jesus Christ. He is the true God and eternal life. (1 John 5:18-20, ESV)

This force that now operates in our world under the nature of the enemy is called "entropy"—where everything left alone is moving toward destruction. We are living in a world that is characterized by steal, kill, and destroy. With entropy, everything declines into disorder, falls apart, or is destroyed. This certainly operates on a global basis in declining cultures, government grabs for powers, oppressive societies, economic failures, awful living conditions, etc. This applies to physical things (even steel and iron bridges), organizations, governments, businesses, relationships, and marriages. (According to *Christianity Today*, February 14, 2014, 30 percent of all marriages—Christian and non-Christian alike—in the U.S. wind up in divorce.) Many more Christian marriages are in a state of separation, and many families are in a state of dysfunctional dynamics. Everything around us is moving toward not working and becoming more difficult. This is ironic in that technology is supposedly exploding to make things easier for us, but that, too, because of steal, kill, and destroy (anyone heard of hacking and viruses?), also is contributing to this spreading destruction. We live in a world of entropy, and none of us can escape it, which is why Paul says we are not just dealing with flesh and blood but powers and principalities.

Remember, the enemy is finite and is not omniscient, omnipotent, nor omnipresent. So how does he and the demonic work? Satan's system operates in a hierarchy. The demonic at your personal level is particularly interested in thwarting God's will in your life by having you exercise your self-will and not follow God's will. (This is the same as with Adam and Eve.) They do this through wiles or schemes (Ephesians 6:11). They are developing these strategies by observing you and your life. Because of our sinful nature, we already are geared toward making poor choices, living in the self, being away from God and His will for our lives, and being easily drawn to sin and the nature of the world. Our propensity is to follow our selfish desires and thus, we are enticed to the things of the world that lead to destruction and the consequences of sin. Further, as we follow our selfish, sinful behavior, the enemy notices cause and effect (i.e., which things cause you to avoid spending time with God; which things get you angry; which things lead you to worry or be anxious; which things bring you fear; who you choose not to forgive; what causes you to over-react; what drives you to look at pornography or to drink, or to be addicted to some other physical thing, etc.).

As these demons observe these cause and effect relationships, they work to create more of the causes so that the effects get deeper and more often—developing what are called patterns, or what psychologists call wounds. Interestingly, the harder you try to overcome these patterns and wounds on your own (self-will), the more you fail, the worse they get, and the deeper they get. Eventually, you resign yourself to these behaviors, and the enemy takes you farther into other areas of new patterns, like guilt and failure. This is all out of his nature of steal, kill, and destroy—creating a world of entropy and a work of thwarting your life.

Entropy is a force that is universally working everywhere in the world—meaning that everything (organic, dynamic, and inorganic) left alone is moving toward destruction. This is why relationships left alone will move toward destruction (separation and conflict). Note the divorce statistics I noted above. This is true for everything. Several years ago, for example, a concrete and steel bridge in Minnesota collapsed. Nothing external caused the collapse, it wasn't struck by something or destroyed by extreme weather. It simply collapsed over time after decades of disregard. As a nation, we are faced with a crisis of a decaying road infrastructure. The roads, which are made of concrete, are being destroyed faster than we can keep up with replacement and repair. Why? Because they are being left alone, with no one monitoring, inspecting, or repairing them. Everything left alone goes to destruction. Imagine boarding up your beautiful home, attaching plywood over the windows, locking the doors, and never setting foot on your property or inside your home for 10 years. Can you imagine what it would look like after sitting unattended for 10 years? Even if no external force affected your house, it would be ruined, destroyed, and on its own path toward entropy. There is no way around it. The same is true for our world. Because it is under the control of the enemy, it is on the path toward entropy.

As we consider our marriages and relationships in life (with which we live every day and are the key to life every day), the enemy works to bring division and separation that: steals, kills, and destroys. The following verses explain that the enemy uses our self (flesh) to bring judgment toward each other and thus, separates us spiritually from our mate. This brings division, which is completely against God's nature and will. We ultimately wind up at enmity against God's will and separate from the life of Christ. Should we allow our relationship to be characterized by division, separation, and arguing, the consequences are severe. There is nothing the enemy would like more than to cause separation in our marriages and friendships. Each of us has to remain on guard for Satan's attack. When he separates us, he does the very things that the Lord despises the most.

First, we see this clearly in Proverbs 6:16-19:

> ¹⁶There are six things that the Lord hates,
>   seven that are an abomination to him:
> ¹⁷haughty eyes, a lying tongue,
>   and hands that shed innocent blood,
> ¹⁸a heart that devises wicked plans,
>   feet that make haste to run to evil,
> ¹⁹a false witness who breathes out lies,
>   and one who sows discord among brothers. (**Proverbs 6:16-19, ESV**)

God says He hates division and those who sow discord (those who continually argue and are not willing to work toward resolution and agreement); and He considers discord an abomination—an atrocity, a disgrace, a disgust, an abhorrence—something truly distasteful to God. We need to receive the severity of His view toward continual discord and division (which the enemy will work overtime to create and keep active). Thus, we are not called to live this way, and understand it is not of God but a wile, or scheme, of the enemy. Of course, natural disagreements are normal in any relationship (we will discuss later); it's the continual strife and discord that God so despises.

Then, in Romans 8:5-8 we see why and how the enemy keeps us in discord and strife.

> [5] For those who live according to the flesh set their minds on the things of the flesh, but those who live according to the Spirit set their minds on the things of the Spirit. [6] For to set the mind on the flesh is death, but to set the mind on the Spirit is life and peace. [7] For the mind that is set on the flesh is hostile to God, for it does not submit to God's law; indeed, it cannot. [8] Those who are in the flesh cannot please God.
> **(Romans 8:5-8, ESV)**

The enemy uses the same deception that he used with Adam and Eve to keep us in conflict: He appeals to us living in the "flesh" or to our "self-will," which we use to make our own decisions without considering God, and particularly not considering our spouse or others in decisions. There are three consequences when we operate this way: death of the Spirit, enmity against God, and a God who cannot be pleased.

When we experience death of the Spirit (as believers who have the Holy Spirit—we are like Adam and Eve, who lost the Spirit from their essence), we basically shut off the power and relationship of the Spirit.

When the Spirit is killed, we experience enmity against God and are working against the will of God—and instead have the Father as an enemy. (How is that going to work for you?)

When we are living in this carnal state, we cannot please God. Displeasing God invites discipline (because He wants us to live in beautiful relationship with Him and receive all the benefits of the abundant life of the Kingdom).

In essence, we go back to the position of Adam and Eve when they sinned. We put to death the Spirit (even though we have the Spirit, we operate as though we do not), we are at enmity against God, and cannot please God. This is why we are continually in disagreement and at odds with each other. We are actually working against God as He attempts to resolve our differences and conflict, and thus, go deeper into discord. As noted earlier, this is something He hates and finds an abomination. This is why Satan works so hard to keep us in the flesh: to deepen our pattern of discord, which, in the flesh, we have no ability to resolve.

James 4:11 helps us to understand another ploy of the enemy that keeps us in conflict: judging.

> [11] Do not speak evil against one another, brothers.[a] The one who speaks against a brother or judges his brother, speaks evil against the law and judges the law. But if you judge the law, you are not a doer of the law but a judge. **(James 4:11, ESV)**

When we judge others, and especially those close to us (like our spouse or close friends), we are setting ourselves up as their judge, instead of letting God be the judge. We are saying, "I am right, and either you are wrong or I don't care what you think; I expect you to do what I want you to do, because I have 'decided' (judged) what is right, and you have no say in this 'case.' I have not gone through 'due process' (working together to come to a resolution or seek God's answer—His judgment), but have become the judge myself." (The decision has been made, and I am right.)

James 5:9 makes this point clear:

> [9] Do not grumble against one another, brothers, so that you may not be judged; behold, the Judge is standing at the door. **(James 5:9, ESV)**

When I set myself up as judge, I am the one who is actually judged. My judgment then becomes my own condemnation, because I am then separated from the fellowship of God. I have put to death the Spirit and am at enmity against God and therefore, cannot please God. The enemy uses the tool of judgment to enable you to operate in the flesh. When we decide for ourselves that we are right, we are then unwilling to go through the process of resolving conflict and disagreement or work together to seek God's will.

Galatians 5:1-4 says:

> For freedom Christ has set us free; stand firm therefore, and do not submit again to a yoke of slavery.
>
> [2] Look: I, Paul, say to you that if you accept circumcision, Christ will be of no advantage to you. [3] I testify again to every man who accepts circumcision that he is obligated to keep the whole law. [4] You are severed from Christ,

> you who would be justified[a] by the law; you have fallen away from grace.
> **(Galatians 5:1-4, ESV)**

In Galatians, Paul makes the argument that if you bring one judgment or law or rule (I am right on this, and you need to follow what I say on this one thing), we actually become obligated to obey the entire law. Which is why, based upon James 5:9, we bring condemnation upon ourselves. What is our ability to obey the entire law? Zero. Zip. Nada. What is the consequence of this? We are separated from the power and relationship with Christ (death of Spirit) and fall from grace. In essence, we are forced to rely on our own flesh and are required to live perfectly. Since this is not possible, we will lose all spiritual power, live in the world controlled by Satan, and suffer negative circumstances, oppression, lack of joy, lack of peace, lack of freedom, and missing the abundant life.

This issue of judging, particularly in normal conflicts and disagreements, can easily be turned by the enemy to discord and division—a serious issue of life. As noted earlier, God hates this and to Him is an abomination—it is created by us living in the flesh under self-will where we put to death the Spirit (allowing our life in the Spirit to die), are at enmity against God and ultimately, cannot please God. We ourselves are then judged and condemned—separated from the fellowship of Christ and fallen from grace/the favor of God. This is why the enemy is working overtime in the lives of believers to create this discord so that we are not living the wonderful life that God has planned—and why abiding is so critical to us. When abiding, we learn how to overcome this wile, this strategy of the enemy who is so very active in this world of entropy.

So, we see that the enemy's plan is to steal, kill, and destroy, especially to divide and separate us as couples and/or from other close relationships and friendships. By having us operate in the flesh, the enemy uses our own self determination to separate us from the power of God. The dynamics of living in this world mean that entropy is everywhere and everything is moving toward destruction. We will face this constantly throughout this life where things are normally going to be difficult—unless we learn that we have a better way with God. We should not be surprised at the destructive nature of the world.

Nevertheless, there is GOOD NEWS (the Gospel)! These difficult things are in no way to keep us from living out the grand life of God, as His plans for our future are always perfect. He has provided a way for us to not be consumed by this entropy, this destruction, the wiles of the enemy—but instead actually be restored back to the exceptional life originally planned for all mankind (though not perfect since we are living in a fallen world). How? **Through Christ, our redeemer, our restorer!**

Though the world has been lost to destruction under the control of the enemy, and our nature is now a sin nature, dominated by self, the Father has given us a redeemer who can bring us back to the beautiful, restored life God intended. Redemption is not just a ticket to heaven, but a restoration of the original life first intended by God in the Garden of Eden.

In John 10:10, the words spoken by Christ are the same words used by the Father in Genesis 1:31 when God looked at His creation and all that He created was exceptionally, super-abundantly good.

"I have come to give life, and give it super abundantly!"

This life that Christ has come to give us, is the exceptional, super abundant, good life originally intended in the Garden of Eden. His death and resurrection conquered death and Satan, and thus, we do not have to live under the control and influence of the destructive enemy; but, rather, we can reverse the destruction and receive what He has come to GIVE—this super-abundant life. This will not mirror the perfection Adam and Eve experienced since they lived without entropy in a perfect place of creation, without a sinful nature that had to struggle with the flesh and issues of the self; but we can experience what He will give us super abundantly.

Christ defines this super abundance in the first public statement of His ministry and as recorded in Luke 4:16-21. Here, He reveals why He has come:

> [16] And he came to Nazareth, where he had been brought up. And as was his custom, he went to the synagogue on the Sabbath day, and he stood up to read. [17] And the scroll of the prophet Isaiah was given to him. He unrolled the scroll and found the place where it was written,

> [18] "The Spirit of the Lord is upon me,
> because he has anointed me
> to proclaim good news to the poor.
> He has sent me to proclaim liberty to the captives
> and recovering of sight to the blind,
>   to set at liberty those who are oppressed,
> [19] to proclaim the year of the Lord's favor."
>
> [20] And he rolled up the scroll and gave it back to the attendant and sat down. And the eyes of all in the synagogue were fixed on him. [21] And he began to say to them, "Today this Scripture has been fulfilled in your hearing." **(Luke 4:16-21, ESV)**

We know that Christ has come to give us super-abundant life. He received this scroll from Isaiah 61 and read verses 1-4. He then applied the truths to Himself saying that He has come to restore this super-abundant life to us now through the good news, the Gospel! When He sat down, He stated that this has now been fulfilled; that what He had come to do had actually begun, and that it now applies to us personally since He lives within us. The super-abundant life is available to us as we learn to abide and receive it. Isaiah 61:1-4 says:

> The Spirit of the Lord God is upon me,
>   because the Lord has anointed me
> to bring good news to the poor;[a]
>   he has sent me to bind up the brokenhearted,
> to proclaim liberty to the captives,
>   and the opening of the prison to those who are bound;[b]
> [2] to proclaim the year of the Lord's favor,
>   and the day of vengeance of our God;
>   to comfort all who mourn;
> [3] to grant to those who mourn in Zion—
>   to give them a beautiful headdress instead of ashes,
> the oil of gladness instead of mourning,

> the garment of praise instead of a faint spirit;
> that they may be called oaks of righteousness,
>   the planting of the Lord, that he may be glorified.[c]
> [4] They shall build up the ancient ruins;
>   they shall raise up the former devastations;
> they shall repair the ruined cities,
>   the devastations of many generations. **(Isaiah 61:1-4, ESV)**

No matter what has happened to us or what situation we are in currently, or what kind of difficulty we are in currently, or what kind of adversity or pressure we are in currently, the good news means that God can help us now. God can restore things now. God can provide His promised super-abundant life now and bring resolution to the things we are facing now! Nothing is too difficult for Him, and we are not relegated to second, third, or hundredth best. He can make all things work together for good for His very best now; the good news is that the super-abundant life is available NOW, not later, or as many of us think, after this lifetime.

He speaks specifically to the conditions that tend to characterize our lives from things we have experienced or are experiencing now—for these He brings the good news of the super-abundant life that He promises. Let's review one by one the promises of Isaiah 61:1-4.

Healing for the Brokenhearted:

The reason people become broken hearted is that the expectations they held for their own lives have not been met. They have drifted into mediocrity or, even worse, are resigned to a life of difficulty or failure. Remember that this is common as we live in a world of entropy where things don't work out as we had planned. However, Christ says that He wishes to heal and restore us into the exciting lives that He has planned, where we will be full of hope and encouragement and will no longer live in broken heartedness.

Release for Those Held Captive:

Over time, we become captive to the patterns we develop that we have tried to overcome but have failed. These patterns have been developing since childhood and are caused by our responses to situations and events. When something happens, we automatically move to fear, anger, anxiety, addictions, etc. When we try to overcome these patterns on our own and we fail, those patterns actually only deepen, and only serve to place us in a captivity from which we cannot escape. Christ promises to bring us freedom from such captivity by releasing us from these patterns and transforming our nature. He will not have us "manage" the pattern but rather will eliminate it. This is true freedom, as there is no more captivity to it.

Gladness for Those Who Mourn:

We mourn because we have lost somebody or something. And when we lose something, our belief is that it is gone and unrecoverable, so we mourn. As we consider our current lives, it is likely that we have lost much and are mourning what we have lost because we are believing that it cannot be restored. Christ, however, promises that He can restore it and will bring us comfort by bringing hope and excitement again.

Beauty for Those Things Once Thought Worthless:

Think about what we do with ashes in a hearth or in a campfire. We throw ashes out because they are worthless. They have no value. In this stage of our lives, oftentimes we have ruined things and made things worthless, like ashes. We typically have discarded them and considered that there's no way we can restore anything from what we've ruined. However, Christ said that He is so sovereign and so powerful that He can turn ashes into beauty. So those things that have been ruined can be restored to beautiful things. This is an amazing truth that brings us an exciting proposition: The future is full of wonder and excitement; and it doesn't matter what has happened in the past, in particular to things that we have ruined ourselves.

Hope for Those Whose Heaviness Feels Unsolvable:

Oftentimes, we cannot see that exciting future or possibility of wonder because a spirit of heaviness hangs on us like a wet wool coat. The heaviness comes when those things pressing on us seemingly have no solution. Everything feels impossible; we feel stuck. As a result, we have heaviness, discouragement, oppression, pessimism, and little hope. We keep working, and nothing changes. This is when we must remember that our hope rests in Christ, because He not only will bring solutions but also will bring the spirit of praise. You will find that things will work because He will make them work! Hallelujah!

Jesus summarizes His promises by assuring us that He will deal with the issues of life that are resultant of the world of entropy and the work of the enemy. The super-abundant life is not a life of helping us manage these issues better or experiencing victory every now and again, while continually suffering through failure other times. He is instead offering true transformation: healing, liberty, beauty, joy, praise, true rebuilding—everything that characterizes the entirety of life. It will take time, but we will be transformed and will live the super-abundant lives that He has come to give us. This is His promise to us. Our role is to learn how to abide in the Vine and receive His fruit, more fruit, much fruit. What a privilege!

The key issue is that as we live in enemy territory, we can either suffer the consequences of entropy that steals, kills, and destroys everything in its wake AND be subject to the wiles of the enemy that is working non-stop to destroy us and have us live in mediocrity, particularly through division and separation of relationships/marriages; OR, we can choose to abide and live out God's plan of redemption and exceptional abundance; and be restored from what has already been hurt and ruined; and the good news—the gospel—is that it is always NOW. Hallelujah.

Let's see what this means in the next chapters.

EXCEPTIONAL LIFE IS A FRUIT.

NOW LET'S EXPLORE
WHAT EXACTLY THIS FRUIT IS.

SECTION 3:
HOW THE FRUIT OF ABIDING
FULFILLS GOD'S PLAN

CHAPTER FOUR
How Can We Live a Life of Forgiveness?

The first fruit we wish to explore is Forgiveness. This is critical to any child of God wanting to live the exceptional life. Because we live in a fallen world, with self-centered, sinful people, we will always be in relationships that will encounter conflict, hurts, and opposition where others cause and deserve our anger and natural un-forgiveness. This is especially true in marriages and close relationships. Yet God calls us to live a life of forgiveness at all times and toward everyone. We can't do this on our own, but can receive this as a fruit of abiding.

In Romans 8:1-2, we learn:

> There is therefore now no condemnation for those who are in Christ Jesus. [a]2 For the law of the Spirit of life has set you[b] free in Christ Jesus from the law of sin and death. (**Romans 8:1-2, ESV**)

Condemnation means punishment, to receive what is deserved—a sentence due to judgment. The recipient of this judgment stands guilty and thus is condemned. For those who are in Christ, there is no condemnation because we have been forgiven. We have been released from our deserved punishment, not because we did something to earn it, but rather because Christ stood in our place and received the punishment Himself. He forgave us based upon His own nature, one of love and forgiveness. He is Love. He is forgiveness. His nature of forgiveness is a beautiful fruit to receive as a primary way of living in the exceptional life He has planned for us. These verses state that in Christ, there is no condemnation. What it does *not* say is that Christ does not condemn us—leaving others and even ourselves who could condemn us. It says *in Christ* there is no condemnation, which means that Christ does not condemn us AND that others do not have the right to condemn us. Similarly, we do not have the right to condemn others. We are to live in forgiveness toward others—every time and all the time—regardless of what they have done to anger or hurt us.

This is what tends to trap us. We confuse forgiveness with reconciliation, as we often allow ourselves to think condemnation is acceptable to those who have hurt or angered us—because in our mind, they deserve it. Think of when the forgiveness by Christ was accomplished. Once and for all, finished, completed at the Cross. Has He offered up His own life so that we might be forgiven? Yes. When? At the cross when He said: "It is finished," and as He sat down at the right hand of the Father, never to repeat this again.

You can review this entire discussion in Hebrews 8-10 where we see that forgiveness is for everyone! His nature and His love are forgiveness.

However, is everyone reconciled to God? No. Why not? Because in order to be reconciled with God, it requires two parties: Christ, with His forgiveness already completed and now freely offered, based on His nature, which we did not deserve, and we who are separated from Him because of our sin nature AND imperfections. We all now have to process that truth that He stood in our place and took on the punishment that we deserved. He who stood in our place did nothing to deserve it. We, who did deserve the punishment, must process this truth and believe that He died in our place and was resurrected. Then, we must receive Him as our Lord and Savior. We, at that moment, are reconciled to Him and forever will spend eternal life with Him.

Again, have all been forgiven? Yes. Have all been reconciled? No. Does He allow those who do not process the truth to remain un-reconciled and live eternally separated from Him (literally in hell)? Yes. Why? Because, though He has forgiven them, He cannot reconcile to anyone that is not willing to process and choose the truth. Christ requires that for someone to be reconciled with Him, a person must believe that God so loved the world that He gave His only beloved son, and whoever believes that Christ died for him and was resurrected shall be reconciled and receive this forgiveness, and not be condemned (John 3:16-18); and that Christ is the way, the truth, and the life, and no one comes to the Father except through Him (John 14:6). If a person does not believe this, he stands condemned and passes into eternity (though as shown in 2 Peter 3:9, it is not God's will) separated from Christ to live in hell permanently. God will not alter the truth for the sake of reconciliation. So, even though Christ has forgiven everyone, we must be reconciled of our own will. Christ cannot alter the truth.

Everyone stands condemned (John 3:18) because of the sin nature (self) and is required to be perfect to be in relationship with a perfectly Holy God. None of us is perfect and all fall short of the glory of God (Romans 3:23). Christ forgave everyone at the cross and offers reconciliation to all freely—with the only requirement being a choice of the will—belief (John 3:16-18). If someone does not exercise his will and process this truth and receive the forgiveness already fulfilled, then they are not reconciled: forgiven, yes, but not reconciled. Remember there are two different aspects of the process. God is forgiveness based upon His own nature; but reconciliation requires two (God's forgiveness PLUS your choice for reconciliation) based upon the truth; and God cannot alter the truth in order to achieve reconciliation.

So, when others hurt, oppose, or come against us, they deserve our anger and condemnation. However, as a believer, we are called to live in forgiveness always. Forgiveness is the place where, with the nature of Christ, we release the carrying of bitterness and condemnation toward another person, based on what Christ has done for us. This is between me and God only, not between me and the person who has hurt me. It frees my heart from carrying the burden of being hurt, the heaviness of constantly thinking about the hurt, and being trapped by unforgiveness.

Let's work to understand this profound concept further.

Christ wants us to operate as He does and calls us to forgive everyone, 100 percent of the time, all the time, and then be available to process the truth toward reconciliation, if the other party is willing to engage in that process. If they are not willing to process truth, we still can live as Christ does—without reconciliation. If we are living in forgiveness, we are always willing to process the truth, even if it takes weeks, months, or years. We also can live in the freedom of whatever level the other party is willing to set toward reconciliation.

Of course, one relationship that requires our devotion toward reconciliation is with our spouse. We will cover this in our next session regarding unity.

Some keys in processing reconciliation can be found in Matthew 5:21-26

> [21] "You have heard that it was said to those of old, 'You shall not murder; and whoever murders will be liable to judgment.' [22] But I say to you that everyone who is angry with his brother[a] will be liable to judgment; whoever insults[b] his brother will be liable to the council; and whoever says, 'You fool!' will be liable to the hell[c] of fire. [23] So if you are offering your gift at the altar and there remember that your brother has something against you, [24] leave your gift there before the altar and go. First be reconciled to your brother, and then come and offer your gift. [25] Come to terms quickly with your accuser while you are going with him to court, lest your accuser hand you over to the judge, and the judge to the guard, and you be put in prison. [26] Truly, I say to you, you will never get out until you have paid the last penny. **(Matthew 5:21-26, ESV)**

To live in forgiveness means that we always have to be willing to ask others to forgive us when we have hurt them and immediately become reconciled back to them when we have caused them offense. Never be too proud to immediately get things resolved. The longer we wait, the more difficult it becomes to bring relationships back to wholeness.

I am reminded of a family who was plagued for nearly seven decades because two members of the family refused to forgive. A young, newly married bride came home one day to find her new sister-in-law wearing her wedding shoes. She not only was wearing them that moment, but apparently had worn them throughout that day, to work, to shop, to lunch. There were obvious signs of wear, but the sister-in-law didn't understand what the issue was. "The wedding is over!" This enraged the young wife. Her anger was so great, in fact, that it tarnished her thinking of the teenaged shoe thief for many years, indeed decades. The husband tried to bring reconciliation but was torn between his sister and his wife. The feud lasted so long that the wife's children, and then grandchildren, learned the tale and it grew so big that the family could never return to fullness. This is a true story about something simple, but there are many more stories that are far more heartbreaking and understandably more difficult to reconcile. I am thinking of those in close relationships who are dealing with adulterous affairs, addictions, lying. But the point is this: We are called to forgive, and to live in forgiveness at all times and toward everyone, regardless of whether the contentious deed is big or small. In our abiding, the fruit of forgiveness will be granted.

In 2 Corinthians 5:12-21, the point continues:

> [12] We are not commending ourselves to you again but giving you cause to boast about us, so that you may be able to answer those who boast about outward appearance and not about what is in the heart. [13] For if we are beside ourselves, it is for God; if we are in our right mind, it is for you. [14] For the love of Christ controls us, because we have concluded this: that one has died for all, therefore all have died; [15] and he died for all, that those who live might no longer live for themselves but for him who for their sake died and was raised.
>
> [16] From now on, therefore, we regard no one according to the flesh. Even though we once regarded Christ according to the flesh, we regard him thus no longer. [17] Therefore, if anyone is in Christ, he is a new creation. [a] The old has passed away; behold, the new has come. [18] All this is from God, who through Christ reconciled us to himself and gave us the ministry of reconciliation; [19] that is, in Christ God was reconciling[b] the world to himself, not counting their trespasses against them, and entrusting to us the message of reconciliation. [20] Therefore, we are ambassadors for Christ, God making his appeal through us. We implore you on behalf of Christ, be reconciled to God. [21] For our sake he made him to be sin who knew no sin, so that in him we might become the righteousness of God.

As we live in forgiveness, our primary role is to be ambassadors. We are to continually offer reconciliation toward those who are not living in wholeness and the full life of Christ, particularly those who have angered, hurt, or opposed us. Remember that reconciliation takes two parties, so our role is strictly to offer the opportunity to process truth out of our heart of forgiveness on the same basis that we have been forgiven (Christ's nature). If the other party does not wish to reconcile or process the truth, we must and can live with this in freedom and peace of our own soul. Our first role is to have forgiveness in our heart so that none of their offense toward us traps us in a life of hardness, wrath, bitterness, or obsession as these destroy our lives of freedom in Christ.

Admittedly, this sometimes can be difficult in family situations where we have attempted reconciliation, but our close relatives (mothers and fathers, for example) will not process the truth or continue to keep hurting us or attempt to keep controlling us with unhealthy schemes (called dysfunctional family dynamics). The question is how best to handle this since we are not called to reject them (especially to honor our father and mother), yet not to be trapped by them while we live in forgiveness. This really can be tricky. In these scenarios, we may be called by God to establish boundaries that are prudent for us not to allow them to continue to hurt us while we honor them in healthy ways.

Remember, we are always called first to live in forgiveness (on the same basis we have been forgiven—through Christ's nature, not on what we deserve). Work hard not to engage in their unhealthy behavior for short periods of time and not be drawn into their anger or unhealthy behavior that causes us to be hurt or respond in unhealthy ways ourselves. Decide when and how often you can get together; and then, when you do get together, pray for strength and power in the Holy Spirit not to be drawn into the games being played. Pray that your heart will look at your time together as a positive time and pray for ways you can bring goodness to this time, regardless of how the family is acting.

Further, pray that your heart will not receive the arrows that hurt you during this time together. When you leave, let it all go, and do not allow un-forgiveness to creep in, but focus on your wonderful life and what is next for you. Stay true to your boundaries and realize that this is the most healthy way to live. It also is God's prescription for you to enable a semblance of reconciliation to occur when the other parties are not really willing to process truth.

Another key element of not living in condemnation is to forgive ourselves. We often tend to remain living in guilt because of our past mistakes. We keep living in the past because of this burden. And yet, we could be free of this burden should we heed Christ's words. Christ says there is no condemnation, and He has fully released us from these mistakes.

In Philippians 3:11-15, we are reminded that we must press forward, forgetting what lies in the past.

> ...[11] that by any means possible I may attain the resurrection from the dead. [12] Not that I have already obtained this or am already perfect, but I press on to make it my own, because Christ Jesus has made me his own. [13] Brothers, I do not consider that I have made it my own. But one thing I do: forgetting what lies behind and straining forward to what lies ahead, [14] I press on toward the goal for the prize of the upward call of God in Christ Jesus. [15] Let those of us who are mature think this way, and if in anything you think otherwise, God will reveal that also to you. **(Philippians 3:11-15, ESV)**

Paul, in his wisdom, states one very important principle that is critical in living the exceptional life in Christ: that we are to forget the past and move on to the high calling of Christ Jesus. This may be an area where God may be calling you to abide and receive the fruit of forgiving yourself so that you can release yourself from past mistakes and fully move forward into the freedom of His plans for you. This is an important part of living without condemnation.

To put this into perspective, I think about a GPS. When we get off track, the device immediately says to make a legal U-turn, which is equivalent to repentance. However, if we continue to believe that we know better and go farther away from the original track, the GPS will tell us that it is recalculating our route to get us back to the original destination. This is the beauty of the sovereignty of God. No matter how far away we have moved from His plans for us, no matter what mistakes we have made, He can recalculate based upon where we are now and restore us back to the super-abundant life. We are to forget the past. This is why there is never any lost hope after having made big mistakes—we don't need to live in the second, third, or hundredth best life. Rather our lives can be completely all that God wishes it to be based upon our living in forgiveness and moving forward into His beautiful life for us—which is always available.

Forgiveness of others and ourselves is a key fruit of abiding. Christ *is* forgiveness completely in the past, present, and future. He is the God who is asking us to grab His hand to move forward and to let go of Satan and the past so that He can deliver to you the abundant life. We are to forgive 100 percent of the time everyone who has hurt us or is hurting us as we are forgiven on the same basis.

Do keep in mind these important notes, however. If those who have hurt us are willing to deal with the truth by processing the truth, then we can reconcile either fully or partially. If they are not, then we are to live with not being reconciled and move on. If they are a relative or someone we need to continue to see, then we are to set healthy boundaries. We are to completely let ourselves off the hook and release our guilt once and for all, and never again live in that guilt.

Forgiveness is one fruit born of our abiding. It is to be offered to everyone (including ourselves), all the time, regardless of whether the misdeed is large or small. This is one path toward God's offering of a super-abundant life.

CHAPTER FIVE
What Does it Mean to Live in Unity?

Before we can receive and live the super-abundant life promised by God, we must first find unity with Him. This means we need to work together to come to agreement both with Him and with each other. But this is easier said than done, especially in today's "me" culture where the emphasis is placed solely on self, and unity in most any form has fallen by the wayside. So often, we refuse, or even forget, to consider the perspectives of other groups or people, as our minds oftentimes have already decided. This is where our desire for the super-abundant life serves as a reminder to include God in our plans! While it might not be typical, it can be received as the beautiful fruit of abiding.

In Psalm 133, we see that unity is the place that God commands the blessing of His will on our lives. When God commands it, our circumstances will happen according to the command. So ask yourself: "Why would you not seek unity?"

> Behold, how good and pleasant it is
>   when brothers dwell in unity![a]
> ²It is like the precious oil on the head,
>   running down on the beard,
> on the beard of Aaron,
>   running down on the collar of his robes!
> ³It is like the dew of Hermon,
>   which falls on the mountains of Zion!
> For there the Lord has commanded the blessing,
>   life forevermore. (**Psalm 133, ESV**)

If we come to unity with our spouse, or with others close to us (as this also does apply to leadership, elders, etc.) who are helping us with decisions, and arrive to the place where God *commands* blessing (He doesn't suggest, He doesn't say *perhaps* or *maybe*, but guarantees He will make things happen to bring us blessing. . .what He has planned for restoring to us the exceptional life), why would we not always live there? And thus, receive the fruit of unity?

This is further explained in Ecclesiastes 4:9-12.

> [9] Two are better than one, because they have a good reward for their toil. [10] For if they fall, one will lift up his fellow. But woe to him who is alone when he falls and has not another to lift him up! [11] Again, if two lie together, they keep warm, but how can one keep warm alone? [12] And though a man might prevail against one who is alone, two will withstand him—a threefold cord is not quickly broken. (**Ecclesiastes 4:9-12, ESV**)

Instead of focusing on changing our spouse or friend by asking them to do what we want based on our desires, we are to serve them by assisting them in their search for unity, especially when they are hurting, having difficulty, or struggling. We cannot change them or fix them, but we can help them reconnect to the life of the Vine where Christ can do the restoring and bring them the healing they might need. We are to be their encouragers and helpers, to be on their side, their best cheerleaders. Two are better than one. When one is down, the other is there to lift us up; when things are not going well (cold, lonely), the other is there to warm us up. And a strand of three cannot be broken especially when you consider that God is the third strand. Our strength will not be broken, and our lives will be able to stand all that the world, with its entropy and the wiles of the enemy, will throw at us. Nothing will defeat us.

In Ephesians 4:1-6, we see further evidence that unity is not only between two of us, but combined with the Holy Spirit.

> I therefore, a prisoner for the Lord, urge you to walk in a manner worthy of the calling to which you have been called, [2] with all humility and gentleness, with patience, bearing with one another in love, [3] eager to

maintain the unity of the Spirit in the bond of peace. [4] There is one body and one Spirit—just as you were called to the one hope that belongs to your call— [5] one Lord, one faith, one baptism, [6] one God and Father of all, who is over all and through all and in all. **(Ephesians 4:1-6, ESV)**

We are not to negotiate settlements and reach agreement in the flesh but rather to discover God's will together, and come to unity with God. The wonderful thing about this process is that we can reach unity 100 percent of the time, all the time, because of the promise given to us by God. He will always reveal His will to us. The same Spirit is within me and my spouse or another believing friend. Thus, if we have a willingness to work through the process, He will reveal to both of us His will. That is why He asked us to make every effort (work hard at this) to get to unity with the Spirit. Another beautiful thing about this process is that this agreement is normal and expected.

Remember, though, on our quest for unity, we are to embrace and honor disagreement, to understand that neither of us knows God's will and that together, through the disagreement, we are now to pursue and work hard to receive God's will. Three possibilities for Him to bring resolution will be:

1. for Him to change my heart and see that what my spouse or friend is seeing is in line with God's will.

2. for Him to change my spouse's or my friend's heart to see that what I am seeing is in line with God's will.

3. that neither one of us is seeing what is in line with God's will and more is to be known before we know God's will. We need to keep asking, seeking, and knocking. Instead of arguing and manipulating disagreements, our heart is to work toward unity as we seek God's will together. Remember that God commands blessing. Why would we not work toward that blessing?

Philippians 2:1-6 reveals further why each of us should consider the interests of others while still seeking unity.

> So if there is any encouragement in Christ, any comfort from love, any participation in the Spirit, any affection and sympathy, [2] complete my joy by being of the same mind, having the same love, being in full accord and of one mind. [3] Do nothing from selfish ambition or conceit, but in humility count others more significant than yourselves. [4] Let each of you look not only to his own interests, but also to the interests of others. [5] Have this mind among yourselves, which is yours in Christ Jesus,[a] [6] who, though he was in the form of God, did not count equality with God a thing to be grasped... **(Philippians 2:1-6, ESV)**

Because you are seeking unity in the Spirit with your spouse or significant other, it is important for you to want your spouse or significant other to want to maintain with integrity their position (their interest) until you both see what the Spirit will show you is His will. You do not want them to "cave" or give in to your solution if they are truly disagreeing with the solution. The key, of course, is that both of you must have forgiveness in your heart toward each other, as well as a willingness to be "neutral" (not stubborn in your interest and not care what God's will is, but being open to hearing God's will, even if it is different than your position or desired solution) until you hear what God has to say as He leads you to His will. Then, together, you work through your disagreement to seek God's will with honor and respect. To do that, you will need to create a safe place that allows for a positive discussion about the issues, facts, and perspectives. God's will will be revealed as you continue to process.

Let's look specifically at how to handle disagreements and differences of opinions.

First, remember that it is always okay to disagree and is a part of God's process as you work to reach unity. We see this clearly in Acts 15:1-6.

> But some men came down from Judea and were teaching the brothers, "Unless you are circumcised according to the custom of Moses, you cannot be saved." [2] And after Paul and Barnabas had no small dissension

> and debate with them, Paul and Barnabas and some of the others were appointed to go up to Jerusalem to the apostles and the elders about this question. ³ So, being sent on their way by the church, they passed through both Phoenicia and Samaria, describing in detail the conversion of the Gentiles, and brought great joy to all the brothers.[a] ⁴ When they came to Jerusalem, they were welcomed by the church and the apostles and the elders, and they declared all that God had done with them. ⁵ But some believers who belonged to the party of the Pharisees rose up and said, "It is necessary to circumcise them and to order them to keep the law of Moses." ⁶ The apostles and the elders were gathered together to consider this matter. **(Acts 15:1-6, ESV)**

Once they realized that they weren't going to agree, they decided to head to Jerusalem to find others to help them. Because they knew it was okay to disagree, while they walked together to Jerusalem, they did not stop enjoying their life—the disagreement did not ruin their day, their night, their weekend. They were okay with the disagreement as they knew they could get it resolved and viewed it as we all are to view disagreements—as a time to wait to hear God's will.

In any disagreement, the key is not only what the apostles did with the disagreement, but what they needed to do to solve it. They got together to "consider the matter" and seek God's will together. They would not pre-judge the answer, they would not make up their own mind, and they would not determine on their own who is right and who is wrong, or disregard the other's position. They sat together to "consider the matter" as God took them to unity to hear and receive His will.

Now, how do we consider the matter?

Ephesians 4:15-16 and 4:25-32 remind us that "considering the matter" requires each of us to speak the truth in love. This is not "the" truth but "our" truth, which is all we can offer. We are not to lie to each other by remaining silent when we do not agree. We need to speak up. We are not to attack each other, not exaggerate, not complain, and not use anger or force to get our way. Rather, we are to discuss truth and share our own hearts so it imparts grace to the hearer and gives them permission to speak their truth as you together work to seek God's will. We must approach these conversations always in forgiveness with no edge to us.

All truth should be spoken in love with respect and honor and, again, without anger. While anger is not sin, it can turn to wrath if we let the sun set on our anger. This does not mean that we have to resolve the issue that moment or that night, but instead that we are to have our hearts right with God. Then, we are to go to forgiveness, with each knowing we are okay together and will continue to consider the matter in a respectful and honorable way at a later time.

> [15] Rather, speaking the truth in love, we are to grow up in every way into him who is the head, into Christ, [16] from whom the whole body, joined and held together by every joint with which it is equipped, when each part is working properly, makes the body grow so that it builds itself up in love. **(Ephesians 4:15-16, ESV)**
>
> [25] Therefore, having put away falsehood, let each one of you speak the truth with his neighbor, for we are members one of another. [26] Be angry and do not sin; do not let the sun go down on your anger, [27] and give no opportunity to the devil. [28] Let the thief no longer steal, but rather let him labor, doing honest work with his own hands, so that he may have something to share with anyone in need. [29] Let no corrupting talk come out of your mouths, but only such as is good for building up, as fits the occasion, that it may give grace to those who hear. [30] And do not grieve the Holy Spirit of God, by whom you were sealed for the day of redemption. [31] Let all bitterness and wrath and anger and clamor and slander be put away from you, along with all malice. [32] Be kind to one another, tenderhearted, forgiving one another, as God in Christ forgave you. **(Ephesians 4:25-32, ESV)**

As we work to process our disagreements, God shows us in Ephesians 4:32 specifically that we always are to process with forgiveness, on the same basis that Christ has forgiven us, which is His nature. It is then critical to actually process the disagreement together. This should be done instead while remaining silent (not telling what we actually think, feel, and believe because we disagree) while the other speaks.

In most relationships, we find it easier to just be quiet and "cave" in to the other to avoid the conflict, as this saves the harshness, the rising anger, and the resultant consequences. This is why it's so important to create a safe place for each to be able to work through the process in a healthy way. We are not to let any unwholesome words come out of our mouths (which grieves the Holy Spirit), but instead process with honor, respect, and consideration for the other. This means active listening and being willing to consider the other party's perspective, interest, and what they may contribute to the process as you work together to seek God's will.

Utilize the following process with your spouse or friend in speaking the truth and listening to the truth as you work toward unity with God. Recall one of the issues you noted in the first session and then practice this before the next session.

1. Discuss with each other the true desires of your heart—your dreams— how can each of you assist in fulfilling these for one another?

2. Take a decision or issue identified last night and begin processing (start with one that has not proved to be highly contentious in the past).
    a. Take one issue at a time.
    b. One of you starts and the other listens:
        i. What do you think, feel, and believe about this?
        ii. When done sharing, the other who has been listening repeats back what he/she heard.
            1. Did I get it right? Did I get it all?
            2. If not, go back and repeat the process until the one speaking can say that you got it right and you got it all.
        iii. Repeat the process for the one who listened until he/she can also say that yes, you got it right, and you got it all.

3. Based upon what you have understood together, one of you then offers a solution to the decision or issue. Explain why. The other then

responds with agreement or a different perspective on the answer. Keep it as long as needed until you reach unity or realize with integrity that you still disagree. Say to each other: We just do not know God's will, and we will continue to seek God until He shows us His answer. Keep asking for wisdom (James 1:5-8). Do not argue or debate, but instead allow it to sit and not ruin your afternoon.

When we are still in disagreement and have not come to agreement in the Spirit, we then keep going. Do not give up, do not just decide or "cave," but together go to a process of prayer and ask, seek, and knock to understand, eventually reaching God's will—His answer.

God will show us the path toward mutual understanding, just as He did in 1 Kings 3:5-9:

> [5] At Gibeon the Lord appeared to Solomon in a dream by night, and God said, "Ask what I shall give you." [6] And Solomon said, "You have shown great and steadfast love to your servant David my father, because he walked before you in faithfulness, in righteousness, and in uprightness of heart toward you. And you have kept for him this great and steadfast love and have given him a son to sit on his throne this day. [7] And now, O Lord my God, you have made your servant king in place of David my father, although I am but a little child. I do not know how to go out or come in. [8] And your servant is in the midst of your people whom you have chosen, a great people, too many to be numbered or counted for multitude. [9] Give your servant therefore an understanding mind to govern your people, that I may discern between good and evil, for who is able to govern this your great people?" **(1 Kings 3:5-9, ESV)**

Even though we consider ourselves capable of making decisions, we need to approach every decision as Solomon did: as a little kid needing God to show us the way. Why? Because there is something we do not know about every decision we are to make. We do not know the future or all the dimensions of our decisions. But God does, so we need Him to reveal His will to us. In hearing His will, we need His discernment. We get that by having a sincere heart, which in the Hebrew means a hearing heart, one that is able to hear Him so that we can see the differences between good and evil (things that are God's best and things that will cause us difficulty and hardship down the road) and that we cannot discern with our own logic based on what is known presently. Particularly, since we are in disagreement, we are not to rely on our own limited perspective but rather to keep hearing what He will reveal to us as His will—what He will show us together as we have "hearing" hearts.

Proverbs 8:32-35 shows that as we are seeking His answers and yet do not have full unity, He gives us three specific ways to process: listen, watch, and wait. When listening, ask each other, "What do you hear God saying?" When watching, observe what information, facts, signs, etc. that God brings next as He is directing you to understanding. Always be willing to receive new information or facts that help clarify what you are learning and understanding as you search for the truth of the situation.

> 32 "And now, O sons, listen to me:
>   blessed are those who keep my ways.
> 33 Hear instruction and be wise,
>   and do not neglect it.
> 34 Blessed is the one who listens to me,
>   watching daily at my gates,
>   waiting beside my doors.
> 35 For whoever finds me finds life
>   and obtains favor from the Lord . . . **(Proverbs: 8:32-35, ESV)**

With our spouse or significant other, we are to continue to process what we are receiving and observing. Listen further to what God will say to you, either directly or through others. Watch for the next things that happen or new information that is given. Keep talking through the things that God is showing and how they impact how He reveals His new information and answers to your questions. Wait until you see His answers, and do not get impatient or act on your own. Keep going through the process until you are certain of His answer together in the unity of the Spirit. The key is to be truthful, to be open to any new information, and to be willing to surrender your will to His.

One couple was learning this principle, and had decided to move out of a large downtown city apartment and purchase a house in a suburban town that they researched and both liked. Their children were about ready to enter school (first grade and kindergarten), and they believed it was a good time for them and their children to make the move. So they began looking, with a heart of unity to try to find a home they both loved. After five months of looking they called Linda and me and said: "This unity stuff doesn't work. We try and we try, but as we have looked and looked, whatever one of us likes the other just doesn't, so we never get to unity. Shouldn't we just pick the one that satisfies some of what each of us would like, even if it isn't exactly right for either of us much less both of us?" We advised that they should not, as the process was working exactly how God intended it to work. They clearly did not yet know God's will. We reminded them that God was purposely using their integrity to keep them in check until they came to unity with Him. We also mentioned that God knows that which we do not. We knew that God had the right thing for them and that He would reveal what that was as long as they continued to abide and continued to stick with the process in search of God's will. They agreed and stayed with it. Three weeks later He received a job offer in a different state that was perfect for his career, for their family, etc. They moved, found a wonderful house, joined a wonderful church, and were able to enroll their kids in an outstanding school. God knew what was ahead and used their lack of unity to keep them from making a decision in the flesh so that they would wait for God's perfect timing. They were truly amazed and are certainly teaching others what it means to live in unity and live in God's perfect will. Best and none better!

Proverbs 11:14 and 15:22 offer other reminders:

[14]Where there is no guidance, a people falls,
  but in an abundance of counselors there is safety. (**Proverbs 11:14, ESV**)

[22]Without counsel plans fail,
  but with many advisers they succeed. (**Proverbs 15:22, ESV**)

When you are stuck (you have processed well but do not see any solution and cannot come to agreement because you are holding your integrity), it is often helpful to get third party help from people who will not give you the answer, but instead will walk together with you as you seek God's will. They can offer good questions, a new perspective, a new thought for a solution, etc., and can help move you past the roadblock. Do not ask for their advice, rather for them to walk with you, going through the listen, watch, and wait as helpers. You also may seek the expert advice of a paid counselor, one who is completely neutral, who has expertise to comment or advise on this issue and who has no stake in the outcome. If your spouse is fearful that an investment may be too risky, for example, do not bring in the broker who is selling you the investment (not neutral) but an analyst who is paid to give you the truth of the situation. Never be afraid of new information, especially from experts (note, they do not have to be Christians) who can bring their knowledge to you directly and who are competent and respected for their expertise and neutrality.

If you still believe you need new information or are still feeling stuck or know that others can be helpful, do not be afraid to bring in outside advisers who can help you in the process of seeking God's will. Remember, these advisers are not to tell you what to do but rather to assist you in reaching unity with God in receiving and confirming God's will. There are basically two types of advisers to consider:

1. Godly advisers: ones who are not just going to give you their personal human advice based on their own experiences, but rather are willing to walk with you and seek God's answers and confirm in the Spirit in unity with Him. They will ask you good questions, help you process in prayer, seek God's word, and receive revelation along with you.

2. Technical advisers: ones who are proficient and competent in their field and can offer you expert advice on a particular subject. They must be completely neutral and impartial and have no vested interest in the outcome. They even can be unbelievers as long as they are the best in their field. Usually they are paid for their time.

With either of these advisers, you are asking for outside input to assist you in helping you receive truth, insight, and assistance. These advisers should help provide direction from the Father as another step in the process toward hearing His answer.

As discussed above, it is important that no unwholesome talk comes out of your mouth. As you are practicing healthy disagreement, then, it is important not to drift back into unwholesome arguments. Most couples have learned many bad habits in attacking each other, many having arguments that let their emotions turn into hurtful attacks. Psalm 4:4-5 give us a prescription for how to handle these situations:

> [4] Be angry,[a] and do not sin;
> ponder in your own hearts on your beds, and be silent. *Selah*
> [5] Offer right sacrifices,
> and put your trust in the Lord. **(Psalm 4:4-5, ESV)**

It is normal to be angry in a disagreement, especially if the disagreements are considered sharp. In these situations in the past, you may have developed unhealthy patterns where you attacked each other and let unwholesome words come out of your mouths. This is where we let anger, which is not sin, per se, become sin. These verses give us a prescription for how to deal with high emotion. We are to separate for the moment into different locations so that we can each get our hearts right with God. This stops the escalation, lowers the high energy, and refocuses us back onto the healthy process of seeking God's will together, instead of speaking against each other because of our own defensiveness, hurt, etc. When we do first separate (which we are called to do), remember that we are to go to forgiveness on the same basis we have been forgiven, through Christ's nature. Then ask God to help resettle your heart so that you are back in peace and able to speak the truth in love about the issue at hand. When we are in forgiveness, and have our hearts right with God, we then can come back together and say to each other: "Are we okay to talk?"; and, if so, then go back to the beginning of the process—let's consider, let's speak the truth in love, etc.

As you fully understand the beautiful fruit of unity, your life will truly begin to discover God's will as He leads you into His plan for your exceptional life. Remember that the unity is not a negotiation of two people to reach a settlement, but unity with the Spirit to discover God's will—and this is something to work hard at all the time. Remember the process begins by speaking the truth in love, listening to the truth, wanting to hear and process the truth, and never letting any unwholesome talk come out of your mouth.

Use advisers if you think they can help, and do not short circuit the process out of convenience. Stay true to your hearts. Keep practicing! And remember it is okay to be in disagreement during the process. The more you practice this, the more comfortable you will feel with disagreeing because you know that you are simply waiting to hear or understand God's will, that God will lead you to unity as you discover His will, that there it will be best and none better, and that He will command His blessing. In the meantime, this disagreement will not ruin your night, your weekend, your week, etc. Why would you not live here!

CHAPTER SIX
What Does it Mean to Be Led by the Spirit?

One of the wonderful fruits of abiding is being led by the Spirit. The Father has placed the Spirit within us and is responsible for guiding and leading us according to His will to a super-abundant life.

The Holy Spirit is the third person of the Triune God (the Trinity) who, upon our belief in Christ as our Lord and Savior, indwells us and becomes our direct connectivity to the Father and to Christ. (Ephesians 1:13-14, John 14:15-24). He intercedes for us and thus receives the Father's will for us and is then responsible for communicating that will to us. (Through Romans 8:26-28 we know that all things work together for our good.) This is one of our wonderful privileges to have God living within us, leading, and guiding us.

Romans 8:12-17 is our guide to understanding that it is no longer necessary to live out the Christian life as a failure, falling to the selfish nature and to sin. Rather, the normal life is to be a child of God led by the Spirit. The Spirit removes the pains of bondage and fear and gives us the spirit of Abba Father, which means daddy. We are to be living the life of a toddler who has no cares about the future but rather lives in the moment and is excited about what the moment brings. The heart of a toddler is always excited and always anticipating the wonderful experience of life together with you. We are children of God and thus, children of the King. It reads:

> [12] So then, brothers,[a] we are debtors, not to the flesh, to live according to the flesh. [13] For if you live according to the flesh you will die, but if by the Spirit you put to death the deeds of the body, you will live. [14] For all who are led by the Spirit of God are sons[b] of God. [15] For you did not receive the

> spirit of slavery to fall back into fear, but you have received the Spirit of adoption as sons, by whom we cry, "Abba! Father!" [16] The Spirit himself bears witness with our spirit that we are children of God, [17] and if children, then heirs—heirs of God and fellow heirs with Christ, provided we suffer with him in order that we may also be glorified with him.
> **(Romans 8:12-17, ESV)**

We should never believe it normal to live in the flesh (self), or to live a life of failure and struggle instead of living a life being led by the Spirit, a life of victory and promised abundance. We are to switch our thinking from believing that a once-in-a-while victory is plenty since we usually are struggling with the flesh and failing to be a child of God being led by the Spirit. We must believe that we are to live instead in abundant victory. To do so, though, means we mustn't go back to the flesh (self). We must go to the remedy, which is repentance, so that we can instantly be restored back into fellowship where there is no condemnation, and where we can continue our vibrant life in the Spirit (1 John 1:9; Romans 8:1-2).

As we are led by the Spirit, one of God's primary roles is to bear witness that we are His child, a child of the King, one who has come to give us the abundant life and restore to us exceptional living. He wants us to fully understand our identity as a child of the King and not live under a bondage of fear or worry, but rather to live the life of a toddler—a child who is excited about everyday life and the adventure that our Father has planned for us. We are not to be so concerned about the things of the future but rather to enjoy the beauty of how the Spirit leads us day by day.

John 16:13-15 shows us how the Spirit leads us into this life of abundance.

> [13] When the Spirit of truth comes, he will guide you into all the truth, for he will not speak on his own authority, but whatever he hears he will speak, and he will declare to you the things that are to come. [14] He will glorify me, for he will take what is mine and declare it to you. [15] All that the Father has is mine; therefore I said that he will take what is mine and declare it to you.
> **(John 16:13-15, ESV)**

Imagine you are going to an art museum to take a tour with a guide. Why would you choose to do this when you could easily roam around on your own? Obviously, because the guide knows more than you do and can take you where you need to go and show you what you need to see.

Does the guide take you to the cafeteria, give you a brochure, explain the brochure, and then say good luck? No, he invites the group to join him as he reveals and explains what each artifact means. If we have curiosity and want to ask more questions, a good guide will listen and then answer the questions as we seek to know more.

Because the Holy Spirit is not on a limited hour-long tour, we have endless time to be able to stop as He guides us and ask questions until we fully understand what revelation He is giving us. He also will alert us to things to come, giving us direction regarding the things that we should anticipate, in addition to things we should not pursue. For example, if I told you that today a woman in a bright yellow dress was going to appear and discuss something significant, we would watch for that person and then listen to what she had to say because we were alerted. In the same way the Holy Spirit is going to alert us to things to come so that we pay attention and begin the process down a certain path. As we gain understanding, this gives us great clarity about His will for us as well as what to pursue and what not to pursue. For example, if you were told that your ministry was going to be leading retreats with couples, when opportunities came along to be an elder in the church or lead a certain committee, we would automatically decline because we know where the Lord is calling us.

The Spirit is consistently leading us, and He fulfills this role in three specific ways:

1. He guides us into all truth. The word *truth* here does not refer just to theological truth but to all truth relating to the issues of your life that the Spirit needs to reveal to you. As you are able to receive all the truth about your heart, circumstances, principalities, and powers, as well as other people's motives, etc., you are then able to understand God's will, which is always based on truth. The Spirit guides us and does not leave it up to us to figure things out on our own. Similar to

a guide in an art museum, He does not just hand us an art Bible and tell us to find the art and understand the truths of the art on our own. Rather, we walk with the guide to each painting as he explains the deeper information, and then, as we are curious, we ask questions that the guide willingly answers, so, eventually, we understand more and more. Being guided by the Holy Spirit is wonderful, because we are not on a quick "one-hour" tour. There is no pressure to keep moving to get to the next thing; and since He wrote the book (the Bible from which He primarily guides us) He knows all truth. We will explore further in the next session how this works in our personal life.

2. He tells us of things to come. Since He knows what is ahead for us in our lives, He will alert us of things to come so we are paying attention to the important things He will reveal to us. His revelations may lack detail, but for good reason. If He is too detailed, we likely would either be too passive and think it will just happen (so we then feel it's not necessary to join Him in the process), or we would try to make things happen on our own and get ahead of His timing and His work of bringing about the plan regarding the future path for us. How He does this is to alert us to pay attention to something so that we begin to look for further revelation and input as He guides us into what is to come. As He alerts you, He will then guide you further—step by step—until what He is telling you about the future is fulfilled. All along, He will keep you in an abiding, intimate relationship with Him. This is the very definition of abiding: Stay in a relationship with Him to keep hearing Him and keep being led by Him.

3. He transfers all that is Christ's to you. A beautiful role of the Holy Spirit is to transfer all that is Christ's to you. This includes His nature, His wisdom, His power, His authority, His truth, His love, etc.—all that is His. And the Spirit is to transfer all that to you. As you are being led and are following Him, abiding in the Vine, receiving His Word, experiencing Him, and walking in His will for you, one of the beautiful benefits is that all that is Christ's is transferred to you. This is why it is

so important to realize you are a child of the King and to be led by the Spirit and not the flesh.

As He guides us into His will, He also is faithful, answering our prayers. This is clear as is written in 2 Corinthians 1:18-22:

> [18] As surely as God is faithful, our word to you has not been Yes and No. [19] For the Son of God, Jesus Christ, whom we proclaimed among you, Silvanus and Timothy and I, was not Yes and No, but in him it is always Yes. [20] For all the promises of God find their Yes in him. That is why it is through him that we utter our Amen to God for his glory. [21] And it is God who establishes us with you in Christ, and has anointed us, [22] and who has also put his seal on us and given us his Spirit in our hearts as a guarantee. **(2 Corinthians 1:18-22, ESV)**

All the promises of Scriptures are yes in Christ. There are over 7,000 promises throughout Scripture; and are all available to us as absolutely yes. This means that all followers of Christ, those being led by the Spirit, are to be the recipient of these promises. There is no partiality. Further, the promises never come with a *perhaps* and *maybe* (or yes and no); but are all *yes* in Christ. The key is that we are receiving these promises from Christ as we are being led by the Spirit. We cannot just decide on our own what we want since they are His promises to give. Even though all 7,000 are yes, they are to be given and received as He so chooses according to His will and His timing. But, as He gives them (and He will), we are to receive them and respond with AMEN, which means, I have heard the Promise of God, I understand it is applied to me personally, and I now agree with God and can say with confidence, "SO BE IT. AMEN." We then are to pray that promise with faith, believing it will be fulfilled as He has spoken it to us.

This is an important element of abiding. We are not simply to choose on our own a particular promise in Scripture and say: "Since this is true (and is true per se), I want this to be true for me at this time, in this situation." Or, "This is how I want it to be fulfilled as true and when I want it to be true." Rather, through abiding, we should ask: "Since your promises are true, what do you have to say about this to me at this time in this situation? I am surrendering my will to your will, as I fully understand that you know everything about my situation and about what is important for me; you know what the future holds and what is around the corner; you have a bigger story in mind and have a purpose that you wish for me to join." Thus, you will seek His wisdom, His counsel, and His guidance as He leads you into the promises that He will speak that we can then say Amen to. He will take us into this abiding relationship of hearing, processing, praying, dialoguing, receiving, and being obedient to His instructions—always with a surrendered heart so that we are following Him and His will, which is best and none better!

How do we then access these promises? John 15:7-8 highlights the "if/then" statement.

> [7] If you abide in me, and my words abide in you, ask whatever you wish, and it will be done for you. [8] By this my Father is glorified, that you bear much fruit and so prove to be my disciples. **(John 15:7-8, ESV)**

If we are abiding in Him, and His words are abiding in us, then we can ask what we will, and it will be done for us (this is described as a fruit). As we are abiding in Him, we will be receiving His words. Our role is to stay abiding until his words get inside our soul to the point that we understand them fully, and we believe them.

Also notice that He says *words* and not concepts or principles or ideas. We tend to read the Bible for concepts and principles and then try to live by them on our own strength. The key is that we look at each of the individual words of the verses and get them into our hearts. Thus, there is no substitute for memorization and then staying with it until it becomes clear to us so that we fully believe it. At that point, we can then pray and expect the answer to come.

As we pray, understanding that He has spoken a promise to us, we must meet the two conditions to have Him fulfill the promise:

1. We must abide in Him (continue in the intimate relationship of abiding).

2. We must have His Rhema words (those promises and Scriptures He has spoken specifically to me, personally, regarding my circumstances and life situations) abide in us.

This means I am engaged in Scripture memory, journaling, spending time processing, etc., until I believe and can pray with confidence and know both that it is God's will and that God will fulfill it.

We will spend more time in the next chapter learning how we have His words abide in us. This then alters dramatically how we pray as we then internalize the if/then scenario noted above: If we abide in Him and His words abide in us, we can pray what we wish, and it will happen to glorify Him. He will fulfill His wonderful promises supernaturally in ways that we on our own cannot, and we will bear witness that it was God and not us. So, our prayer life is not giving God a list of things we want Him to do for us or give us; but rather we are seeing His will, and His promises regarding our circumstances and life situations so that we then receive what He has to speak about these. As we hear and understand, we abide in those, pray those, and then see things change in our lives!

One of the wonderful answered prayers arising from the abundant life is God fulfilling the desires of our hearts, as seen in Psalm 37:3-8:

> [3] Trust in the Lord, and do good;
>   dwell in the land and befriend faithfulness.[a]
> [4] Delight yourself in the Lord,
>   and he will give you the desires of your heart.
> [5] Commit your way to the Lord;
>   trust in him, and he will act.
> [6] He will bring forth your righteousness as the light,
>   and your justice as the noonday.
> [7] Be still before the Lord and wait patiently for him;
>   fret not yourself over the one who prospers in his way,
>   over the man who carries out evil devices!
> [8] Refrain from anger, and forsake wrath!
>   Fret not yourself; it tends only to evil. **(Psalm 37:3-8, ESV)**

As we delight in Him (He is delighted by us abiding in Him, spending time with Him, being led by Him, loving Him, trusting Him), He will give us the desires of our hearts. The Father enjoys syncing circumstances in our lives with the desires that are in our souls (part of the essence of us and part of our make up as He created us). They are truly in our hearts so we do not have to try to separate these between "holy and secular." They all are part of the abundant life that He is giving us; and He will refine these desires to reveal what they truly are as we seek to understand them and allow Him to show us what is pure and God honoring versus anything that is self-centered. But let Him show you that, and do not censor those desires since they are in your heart. Remember, this is a life-long "giving" as part of the abundant life for us. We are not to put a timeline on any of it or pursue it on our own, but instead realize that over our lifetime, His heart is to give us the desires of our hearts that thrill us, provide adventure, give us hope and excitement. One of our couples who went through an exercise at a retreat in 2007, as described below, reports the following experience to give you an example of how it has worked for them:

The Desires of Our Hearts for Marriage
John and Michelle Santaferraro

When our marriage hit rock bottom and verged on break up, we knew we had to do everything we could to save it. We decided to attend a marriage retreat. There, Rich and Linda Case taught us about "abiding in Christ" for the good of our marriage and, importantly, they taught us how to do it. Abiding in Christ made sense to us, but we were skeptical about the idea that God would speak to us through His Word and that He would have a special passage for us that could help our marriage.

Despite our skepticism, we decided to give it a try. One verse in the Bible that caught my (John) attention was Psalm 37:4, "Delight yourselves in the LORD, and He will give you the desires of your heart." I decided I should try to unpack this verse further.

On my road toward abiding, I began studying the meaning of the word "delight." I thought it would have something to do with celebration and excitement. But I learned that it actually meant delicate morsels, tender moments, beautiful experiences. This was exactly what I had been wanting in my marriage.

With some of my skepticism behind me, I continued. I wanted to know what the word "desires" meant. When I found the Hebrew definition, it included the word, MISH'ALAH. My wife is Michelle, but I call her Michy [pronounced mishee]. It was as if my wife's name was somehow hidden in the "special word" God had given me. His promise to me was that He would give me the wife of my heart, along with the desires of my heart.

Rich then gave us a challenge. He suggested that Michelle do as I did and ask God to reveal the desires of her heart. We prayed, asked God, and we both started to think about what an exceptional, beautiful marriage might look like.

God answered our prayer. Separately, we each created a list of desires for our marriage. We even wrote down items that excited our hearts personally. Then we came together to journal about these desires, such as making our home together more intimate, and that our marriage would be a beacon of light and hope to those around us. There were 13 total.

I spoke with Rich again, and he instructed me to continue my abiding in Psalm 37. His suggestion was to look at the next verse. If God had given me this passage in the Bible, as Rhema, then He would continue to guide me further through the passage.

The answer to me was clear. Psalm 37:5 says, "Commit your way to the LORD, trust also in Him, and He will do it." My instruction from God was to continue abiding, "Delight yourself in the LORD." Then, regarding the desires of our heart, we were supposed to let God give them to us, "Commit your way to the LORD, trust also in Him, and He will do it."

For the next several months, Michy and I met regularly to pray through the desires of our hearts, and shared with each other anything we had seen God do to bring these things into our marriage.

After about six months, God had done some part of everything that was on our list. God has continued to pour into our relationship the beauty that He designed for our marriage. And, He has continued to build on these desires to take us to deeper, more beautiful experiences for our marriage. We rewarded our abiding in ways neither of us could have imagined.

In the next week or so, write down the desires of your heart—do not censor them by qualifying whether you think they are holy enough—just note whatever you have within your heart (they are there). Then, discuss with your spouse or significant other and let your dreams expand as God gives you the desires of your heart. Remember, He is the one who gives you these, not you chasing them.

To confirm these promises as you pray, remember that we have the privilege of confirmation with others through the Spirit as shown here in Matthew 18:18-20:

[18] Truly, I say to you, whatever you bind on earth shall be bound in heaven, and whatever you loose on earth shall be loosed[a] in heaven. [19] Again I say to you, if two of you agree on earth about anything they ask, it will be done for them by my Father in heaven. [20] For where two or three are gathered in my name, there am I among them." **(Matthew 18:18-20, ESV)**

When you go to another party to confirm, the Spirit will show you agreement. Do we have confirmation in our spirit that we have God's will? If so, He will show it. When you both receive confirmation in the Spirit (through peace, strength of conviction, and when both see what God is showing you), unity is then achieved.

As we pray, God has given us a wonderful and very practical way of understanding what to pray as we seek His will or His promises (what is He speaking to us about our circumstances, situations, etc.). We are to gather in His name as we seek His will and His promises, ask what He wants to speak to us, and then together, with our spouse or other believer(s), go to Unity with the Spirit until we fully and clearly understand His will. This will be confirmed in our spirit through peace and further will be confirmed by the Spirit as we enter into unity that we are hearing and understanding with clarity together. This is where most of your time in prayer is spent—processing until you understand His will. When we do, we then shift to asking God to fulfill what He has spoken as His will—since He promises to deliver it. Further, He gives us the spiritual power to bind the principalities and powers who are opposing God's work and will in our lives (to cause them to cease coming against us); and to loose the mighty power of heaven to fulfill God's promises and bring freedom to our situations. Again, this gives a different paradigm of prayer: not giving God a list, but seeking His will and then, as we understand His will, praying for that will and believing that He will fulfill His will.

When needing further insight from God, we are to continue to pray. James 1:5-8 shows us how:

> [5] If any of you lacks wisdom, let him ask God, who gives generously to all without reproach, and it will be given him. [6] But let him ask in faith, with no doubting, for the one who doubts is like a wave of the sea that is driven and tossed by the wind. [7] For that person must not suppose that he will receive anything from the Lord; [8] he is a double-minded man, unstable in all his ways. **(James 1:5-8, ESV)**

We cannot see the future, but God knows the future, so no matter how much we think we know what to do, we always lack wisdom since what is ahead may impact the decisions that God wants us to make in accordance with His will.

All we have to do when we seek wisdom is to ask for it. There is no condition for how mature we are in our walk with God. He promises to get us the answer in a way we can understand it. He will take on the burden of communicating the answer in ways that are geared toward our ability to receive the answers. Just as you would adjust your communication to a three year old versus a 10 year old, you deliver the answer as they need to hear it. However, there is one important condition to all this: that you believe He will get you the answer. It is not necessary to believe at first what you hear (remember He is the author and finisher of faith, so though what He says may be too lofty or something beyond us, He just says then to stay with Him as He reveals to us that what He says is true).

Keep in mind that it is conditional that you get settled that He will speak and get you the answer. If you aren't settled, then you won't know where the answer comes from: God, the enemy, or yourself. Even if He revealed the answer to you, you wouldn't be confident in it and would still be trying to figure things out on your own. Once you truly believe He will get you the answer, you must then look for, trust, and receive the answer that He gives. Only at that point will it be clear and knowable by you.

SECTION 4:
HOW DO WE ABIDE?

CHAPTER SEVEN
How Do We Abide?

Now that we understand that abiding leads to receiving fruit—more fruit, much fruit—we are to learn to enjoy fully Abiding in the Vine—our relationship in God. Let's explore how to abide. Remember abiding in the Vine is being connected to Christ—in a relationship with Him—through the Spirit. This occurs through the entirety of your life, 24/7, and you will be engaged in this relationship all the time (not just during Bible study or attending church or spiritual functions). It is centered on the Word, since He has written to us His truths and speaks His promises through the Word. Abiding is a relationship and not tasks, and thus, to be enjoyed, to be intimate, to be a wonder, to be growing and loving.

In Luke 10:38-42, we are offered a clear example of what it means to abide.

> 38 Now as they went on their way, Jesus[a] entered a village. And a woman named Martha welcomed him into her house. 39 And she had a sister called Mary, who sat at the Lord's feet and listened to his teaching. 40 But Martha was distracted with much serving. And she went up to him and said, "Lord, do you not care that my sister has left me to serve alone? Tell her then to help me." 41 But the Lord answered her, "Martha, Martha, you are anxious and troubled about many things, 42 but one thing is necessary. [b] Mary has chosen the good portion, which will not be taken away from her." **(Luke 10:38-42, ESV)**

We see in these verses that Jesus was good friends with Martha and Mary (and their brother, Lazarus) and often stopped by on His way to Jerusalem from Galilee. (He would attend the feasts in Jerusalem, but spent most of His ministry in Galilee.) Martha and Mary understood Him as Messiah in their limited view of who that was. During this particular visit, Martha was busy serving Christ. From her perspective, she was doing a wonderful thing—serving the Messiah. She thought these tasks were so important that she asked Mary to help, but Mary stayed put. So, she asked Christ to ask Mary to get up and help. Christ responded by saying, "Martha, Martha, you are worried and troubled about many things." The construct of Jesus' words here reveals that Martha believed she was serving Jesus. Actually, though, she was serving herself. She was working for God but forgot the most important question to God, which was, "What would you wish me to do?"

Jesus explained to Martha that Mary had chosen the better thing by sitting at His feet and dialoguing with Him. She had a made the choice to sit at His feet, entering into a dialogue where they could have intimate conversation as she sought truth, understanding, and clarity. This is the essence of a sweet abiding fellowship with God.

So, even when we decide to do tasks for the church, this may or may not be serving God if we haven't asked Him (through our abiding) what our priorities should be. We are to sit at God's feet, just as Mary had done. Jesus was revealing truth to Mary, and Mary was receiving that truth as she was asking questions, responding, and processing what Jesus was speaking to her. She was abiding. She was in relationship with Him, having wonderful fellowship with Him, and willingly and gladly receiving all that Christ was revealing to—and taking into—her heart. It was her choice—she chose to do the better thing. In other words, this is not automatic or forced, but is something that we must choose for ourselves, in our own lives. There will be time for tasks later.

In Proverbs 4:1-7 and 20-23, we are told several times to pay attention to what is being spoken to us, and then to get those words into the midst of our hearts.

> Hear, O sons, a father's instruction,
> and be attentive, that you may gain[a] insight,
> [2] for I give you good precepts;
> do not forsake my teaching.

> [3] When I was a son with my father,
>   tender, the only one in the sight of my mother,
> [4] he taught me and said to me,
> "Let your heart hold fast my words;
>   keep my commandments, and live.
> [5] Get wisdom; get insight;
>   do not forget, and do not turn away from the words of my mouth.
> [6] Do not forsake her, and she will keep you;
>   love her, and she will guard you.
> [7] The beginning of wisdom is this: Get wisdom,
>   and whatever you get, get insight. **(Proverbs 4:1-7, ESV)**
>
> [20] My son, be attentive to my words;
> incline your ear to my sayings.
> [21] Let them not escape from your sight;
>   keep them within your heart.
> [22] For they are life to those who find them,
>   and healing to all their[a] flesh.
> [23] Keep your heart with all vigilance,
>   for from it flow the springs of life. **(Proverbs 4:20-23, ESV)**

We are to be receivers by paying attention to what Christ is speaking to us and not deciding on our own what we should study. We have to understand that this is not difficult. Instead, we will find that what is being spoken to us will be clear to us in our hearts and come from multiple sources. It could be a theme that we see over and over again, it could be something of high interest to us that we would like to know more about, it could be a quickening of our spirit by something that somebody says or something that we see that we realize God is calling us to go deeper.

Through these verses, we are also reminded that abiding is not Bible study or just doing daily devotions. It is not a simple tasklist to be checked off, one that says, "Yes, I spend a few minutes in the Bible." Rather it is paying attention to what the Lord is speaking to you: where He wants you to "camp out"—where

He wants you to spend days, weeks, even months in the Word so that you can process the power of the living Word until it fulfills its work in your life and transforms you and changes your circumstances through promises given. This means it has to get into your heart, your soul—and this takes time—time to memorize these verses (not a memory program but where the Lord has you abiding), journaling out what the verses are saying and what they mean to you; and how you are responding to what you understand and struggle with about these verses; ask questions, dialogue with God about these truths, seek further understanding about things that seem complex and difficult or hard to believe, and continue to process with these words through insight and revelation from the Spirit until you do believe it, experience it, and the Spirit releases you from it—because it has become part of you. Remember, there is no rush, and no timeline—it may take weeks and even months—but that is okay since He is directing our lives according to His plan for what He wants us to receive.

Proverbs 22:17-21 reinforces these thoughts:

> [17] Incline your ear, and hear the words of the wise,
>   and apply your heart to my knowledge,
> [18] for it will be pleasant if you keep them within you,
>   if all of them are ready on your lips.
> [19] That your trust may be in the Lord,
>   I have made them known to you today, even to you.
> [20] Have I not written for you thirty sayings
>   of counsel and knowledge,
> [21] to make you know what is right and true,
>   that you may give a true answer to those who sent you?
> **(Proverbs 22:17-21, ESV)**

Once you are able to carry the words into the heart (soul) and able to speak them from the heart brings about God's best and deepest abiding trust. There is no substitute for Scripture memory, processing through journaling until the Word is in us and we believe it. The working of the Word is what brings about faith and then God fulfilling His promises to us. It is His role to make the Words known to us. The truth is something that "even you" can receive. Nothing is required except willingness. We are all as able to abide and hear His voice as even the most spiritually mature people. Why? Because our sufficiency comes from Him. The only requirements are a heart to hear, a faithfulness of abiding in the Word, and an understanding that He is speaking to us personally.

As mentioned, abiding takes time. There is no rush, but requires much meditation, pondering, and processing as you dialogue with Him daily and throughout the day as He reveals things to you. Further, you can be assured that God will bring other people along the path so you can share what you are receiving. This is an indicator that you are getting this into your heart, that you can speak it out (without having to go to your notes or even to the Bible). You need not have fully received all the wisdom or understanding of the word that God is giving you, but rather to share whatever it is you have received so far. This is God's way of reinforcing what you are receiving and deepening it within your heart. As you speak it out, what you are learning will actually be being received by you and will give you further insight as to what it means to you and your particular situation.

Let's work through another set of instructions to understand further how to go deeper as you are abiding in the Word.

ABIDING IN THE WORD

There are so many ways to deepen your relationship with God. But here are some good places to start. What interesting Word or thought has the Spirit used to pique your interest; what do you already know God is laying on your heart? It's time to pursue that interest!

How to Abide in God's Word:

Write out the specific Scriptures using a good Cross Reference Study Bible with helps and concordance: NKJV (Spirit Filled Life Bible is particularly good, as it includes translations of Greek and Hebrew words); NASB; NEV; Amplified. Do not use a paraphrased work as a primary Bible, only as some additional help. Go to www.biblegateway.com or www.crosswalk.com for different translations. Spend some time understanding the context of the specific Bible Book from which the verse is taken. Also, do not read just the specific verse, but read the entire paragraph for context.

Cross reference specific verses by using your Cross Reference Study Bible, which will take you to other truths about that particular revelation; and perform Word studies using the concordance at back of your Bible or www. biblegateway.com or www.crosswalk.com. As you spend time in the cross-referenced or Word study verses, let the "quickening" of the Spirit lead you regarding whether this is something He is speaking to you; and only then spend time further processing. If it does not strike your heart much, do not spend any further time on it and continue to cross reference other verses that strike your heart or go to another verse from your Word study.

Write out your thoughts about:
- What this says about the character of God?
- What God has done, is doing, or promises to do?
- Are there any conditions to what God promises? (If…then)
- What are my responsibilities or responses?

Go deeper into Hebrew and Greek meanings of the Words He is speaking to you. At www.studylight.org go to: Study the Interlinear Bible. Put in your Bible Book and then Chapter; then click on Study. The chapter will come up, and then you click on the word you wish to know. On the next screen, all of the Greek and Hebrew word definitions for your word will be displayed. If you wish to go deeper, you can go to Word origins and click on that number and further definitions will be offered.

Memorize the verses (word for word)—carry 3x5 cards with you.

Journal your thoughts:
- Do I believe this in my heart (is it settled)? Why or why not?
- What do I struggle with, and what experiences in my life work against what I am receiving in the Word?
- How do these words apply to my situation and me?
- How is God calling me to adjust my life to Him and His will?
- What thoughts come to me about all this?
- Dialogue with the Father your thoughts. Ask for clarity, understanding, wisdom, faith.

Pray the promises: Ask God to fulfill what He has said to you.

- Commit time with friends of accountability or your spouse and share your journal. What is God saying to you?
- Discuss feelings, reactions, and insights. Process why this is important to you.
- Study specific verses that each is sharing.
- Pray verses together.

As you review this set of instructions, consider some key points:

Write out the Scriptures long hand instead of just reading or copying/pasting from a computer, as this will help you see all the words in the Scripture—the verbs, the if/then statements, each phrase, etc. It will open up your heart to see what the Lord wishes to speak to you.

As you are abiding and maturing in your abiding, do not use a paraphrased version of the Bible because, in this case, you are not reading the Bible, but a person's interpretation of the Bible. This is okay for a brand new believer who is getting used to reading the Bible for the first time, but as you move into abiding, you need to go to a word-for-word or a thought-for-thought translation that stayed true to the original languages.

As you are abiding, you will receive life, a high interest in, or a desire to look further into certain verses that strike your heart. Do the cross-referencing, as described in the instruction sheet. It will lead you to further insight and truth about the very thing the Lord is speaking to you. Continue to journal about what you are led to in the cross-referencing and further cross reference from there. You also may wish to do a word study on a particular word that strikes you and see where else in Scripture this word is spoken and if there is life for you there as well. If you cross reference and there is no life or particular meaning for you, then just pass on it, and do not try to force something. Remember, this is God speaking to you and not a book study or a report, so let it always be life to you.

It is good to write out what the verses actually say so you do not read into the verses but let them speak to you. Follow #4 in the instruction sheet to outline what the verses say.

You can use computer software programs to go to the Greek and Hebrew word meanings, which are quite a bit more precise than English. As you write out the verses, you will see certain words that you wish to know exactly what they mean (and will have great impact on what you receive), so circle those, and then in your abiding time, go to the Greek and Hebrew and learn all that they mean. As you learn this, you will find it to be great fun and very insightful.

Memorize the verses in which you are abiding. Again, no rush, take your time, and just work on memorizing these so they get into your heart.

A key to abiding is your personal journaling—your authentic dialoguing with God about your processing of the truths He is revealing to you. This is not a sanitized version, as if you were going to read it in front of church, but rather just between you and God and what is really going on, including all your frustrations, lack of belief, all of your struggles, etc. This dialogue is then a back and forth dialogue as He moves you to His desire to transform your heart and bring changes in your circumstances according to His wonderful plan for you. The journal is only to be between you and God and no one else, including a spouse. You never hand it to another person (certainly you can share certain things with your significant other, but don't let them read it. This keeps it safe for your authentic heart to be shared with God).

You are to pray the promises and the verses He is giving you.

At least once a week, you are to share with your spouse what God is speaking to you. This will help you understand what God is speaking, and be each other's best cheerleader as you pray for each other and ask God to fulfill what He is speaking.

As we abide in the ways we learned above, there are other key elements to the process. Even though Jeremiah's message was most difficult for him to receive and then proclaim to the nation of Israel, consider how he still enjoyed the abiding he had with God. Jeremiah 15:16 says:

> 16 Your words were found, and I ate them,
> and your words became to me a joy
> and the delight of my heart,
> for I am called by your name,
> O Lord, God of hosts. **(Jeremiah 15:16, ESV)**

This reminds us that we are to "eat" His Words—to ruminate, to ponder, to meditate—not just read or take one pass at His Words, but to spend sufficient time in these Words, so that we absorb them into us (i.e., eat them). Then, as you abide, and as you help your spouse or significant other abide, you should also ask, "Am I enjoying my abiding?" If not, then you have drifted back to the intellect and are trying to do something on your own instead of paying attention to where the Father is speaking to you and giving you life, which is always a joy. We are to enjoy the Words—even when they are challenging, convicting, asking us to repent, etc. because they are leading us to life, and to God's will, which is best. There is none better. If we are not enjoying our abiding, then go back to when you were, restart again with receiving, and not striving, and remembering that abiding is a relationship and not just a study.

Luke 2:41-52 explains a bit about how to process what we are learning and seeing while abiding.

[41] Now his parents went to Jerusalem every year at the Feast of the Passover. [42] And when he was twelve years old, they went up according to custom. [43] And when the feast was ended, as they were returning, the boy Jesus stayed behind in Jerusalem. His parents did not know it, [44] but supposing him to be in the group they went a day's journey, but then they began to search for him among their relatives and acquaintances, [45] and when they did not find him, they returned to Jerusalem, searching for him. [46] After three days they found him in the temple, sitting among the teachers, listening to them and asking them questions. [47] And all who heard him were amazed at his understanding and his answers. [48] And when his parents[a] saw him, they were astonished. And his mother said to him, "Son, why have you treated us so? Behold, your father and I have been searching for you in great distress." [49] And he said to them, "Why were you looking for me? Did you not know that I must be in my Father's house?"[b] [50] And they did not understand the saying that he spoke to them. [51] And he went down with them and came to Nazareth and was submissive to them. And his mother treasured up all these things in her heart.

[52] And Jesus increased in wisdom and in stature[c] and in favor with God and man. (Luke 2:41-52, ESV)

Here, a 12-year-old Jesus was sitting with his teachers, the Pharisees, and the Sadducees. During His ministry He would have challenged these very teachers, questioning whether they had the heart of God. But in this scenario He was a learner, a receiver. He asked questions, He expressed His understanding so that they could take Him deeper, and then He summarized His understandings. We are to have the same approach to abiding with Him. We are free and encouraged to ask questions, to dialogue until we gain understanding, and then to clarify what we do understand. If we use the same process in our abiding, particularly using journaling as a way of recording these thoughts, we will be able to gain understanding and reach clarity on exactly what the Lord is speaking to us.

Remember: As you abide, you are to be listening to what He is speaking to you. Many of the truths you come across should raise up things that you do not understand, or beg the question, "if that is true, then how does this work?" This will draw you further into deeper abiding to discover the answer to the questions. This is a beautiful process: listen, ask questions, write what you know. Keep the process going throughout your journaling.

CHAPTER EIGHT
What Does the Father Have to Say to You?

Now that each of you has learned the wonder, the life, and the joy of Abiding in the Vine—in the vital relationship of Christ through the Spirit as you serve as a Branch and allow the Vinedresser to direct the steps of your life— we wish to end this curriculum by offering a personal experience of abiding. This will be a time of personally hearing from God that will launch you into where the Father wishes you to begin in the Word—your own deep abiding. Remember, this will be a commitment to daily time with Him. It isn't something to rush through or some must-do activity, but a time to receive what He wishes to produce in your life (fruit!). We have been blessed to discover this wonderful process using a place in Scripture. This Scripture is one He uses to speak to each of us personally so that He might reveal all that He has planned for us. Please turn to Ezekiel 34, verse 11 in your cross reference Bible.

In Ezekiel 34, God is speaking to the nation of Israel, His beloved children. The leaders of Israel have not been faithful in shepherding His people—they have been misleading them, not teaching them truth, and leading them astray— away from following God. He tells the leaders to step aside so that He Himself could shepherd the people directly. He would lead them and be their provider, their teacher, and fulfiller of Covenant promises. In verses 11-30, there are 22 "I wills" where God expresses the promises that He is making directly to His children with no conditions. The only implied condition as is always true in Scripture is that we are to hear what He is speaking to us, to receive what He is speaking to us personally, and then believe what He is speaking. (This has proven to be a wonderful place to experience God speaking to us about His promises. Over the years, we have had over 2,000 people go through this exercise. What is truly remarkable is that every single person has received a personal Word from God.)

From one retreat, I am reminded of a woman who arrived rather despondent and sad, indeed heavy hearted. She was a divorcee who had remarried and was attending with her new husband. During our session on forgiveness, she had lots of questions about the difference between forgiveness and reconciliation, especially about how to go to forgiveness when reconciliation was not likely. During this "Ezekiel exercise," the Lord told her to go directly to forgiveness of her ex-husband. In doing so, she would receive freedom. Since she had spent much of the weekend processing this, she believed she had received Christ's forgiveness for her ex and could now move to her own forgiveness of him. The distinction between forgiveness and reconciliation had become clear to her; she no longer was confused between the two. She began to understand that this was between her and God.

We could see a burden lifted from her heart and a new contentment had come over her. At the end of our retreat, over brunch, we shared what we believed to be the one key thing the retreat meant to us (beside what He spoke to us in the Ezekiel exercise). She and her new husband both said they had received the freedom of knowing that she not only could forgive her ex, but that she knew she could now be reconciled with her daughter, whom she had not seen in 20 years since her first husband had taken her away from the family. We were grateful to hear her words but also were amazed when she added, "She lives here in Denver!" Right where we were. Even though she and her husband were to catch a plane home to Chicago, we urged them to stay, to figure this out. She did. The next day, she called to say, "You will not believe what happened today! My daughter found me on Facebook and asked if she could call me. Of course I said yes. She revealed that she is a follower of Christ and that last night He had prompted her to seek forgiveness from her mom for not reconciling and to ask if we could begin a relationship." Of course the mother said yes, and they reunited over a beautiful meal. Her despondent, sad, heavy heart turned into joy and beauty: just as God has promised and had spoken to her personally.

In another retreat, we met with a person who was in charge of small groups at a large church. During our retreat, as we worked to process through how Christ restores to us things that were lost, this gentleman was consumed by questions. None of it coincided with how he saw things. He wondered if what conditions must be met to receive restoration. He questioned whether some were subject to "luck and serendipity," in their quest for restoration? "Shouldn't we just accept those things that were already set in motion, especially if we might have caused those things ourselves?" he wondered. As we all worked through the Ezekiel exercise together, he felt called to repent. If he chose to repent, all would be restored, and he would live out the blessings of the Covenant.

Though we probed him regarding what he understood the repentance to be about and the need for restoration, he was vague. The next day, he called and asked me if he could meet me for lunch right away. I agreed. During our time together, he said: "You said in the Gospel of John 10:10, that Christ has come to provide the super-abundant life. Is that true? And, can that happen now, for anyone, no matter what?" I confirmed that it was indeed true, it is a promise God made to you. "Why don't you fill me in on what is going on," I encouraged. He confessed to me that he was in deep trouble. "I have made a mess of things in my business. And, I made this mess myself." After he explained the trouble, I assured him that God could handle it. He then added more detail to the story, and then more and then more. Each time I assured him that God could handle all of it. Then he added one last detail, to which I jokingly replied, "Okay, everything but that." We both had a good laugh, and then I assured him that God could handle that, too. Indeed, He could handle everything. "But," I asked, "are you willing to go and follow as He leads you? You first will need to repent as instructed. And, then you will need to take each step that He tells you to take. I am betting that will likely mean you must tell all of the truth, no matter what the consequences. You also should not try to manage the outcomes or answers. You must let God guide you step by step until you are fully restored. What He promised He will fulfill."

I learned later that he did as he had been led, and he continued to abide and obey. Within five months, what was impossible for man, was completely restored by God! He was free from the entire problem that he himself caused. God can handle all of it!

Step One:

Go through the 22 verses of "I will" and choose as many as strike your heart. Pay attention to your heart as something that God wants to speak through, and skip over any that do not have this quickening of the spirit. Do not over analyze or try to figure it out intellectually; or worry about whether or not it or they are the "right one(s)." Simply notice which one(s) strike you. Then go back through all the ones you have checked and choose one that particularly strikes your heart at the moment—something that you believe God wishes to speak to you today.

Based on the one you chose, write that verse longhand. Then write what you believe it means to you personally in the context of your life. Do not look it up on the internet, or read what a theologian has written in a commentary about it, or even glance at the notes at the bottom of your Bible. The key is to ask what the verse says to you, in your heart? This is about what you are receiving and understanding—the key to abiding—not about being "right." It should be the beginning of a dialogue with the Father and receiving what you see and perceive (realize this is just the beginning).

Then go to the cross references in the center column from that verse. See where that takes you elsewhere in the Scriptures and read the entire paragraph of that cross reference. As you read that entire paragraph, you again choose a verse that is speaking to you. It may or may not be the exact verse that was listed in the cross reference, but one that strikes your heart. Write out that verse longhand; and then again, as you did with the first verse, write what it means to you personally in the context of your life.

Then go to a third cross reference in the center column from the second verse that you received. Go to where that takes you in the Scriptures and read the entire paragraph of that cross reference. As you read that entire paragraph, you again choose a verse that is speaking to you. It may or may not be the exact verse that was listed in the cross reference, but one that strikes your heart. Write out that verse longhand; and then again, as you did with the first verse, write what it means to you personally in the context of your life.

When you are finished, you should have three verses written out longhand, along with what you wrote about how each verse spoke to you personally in the context of your life.

Step Two:

Now that you have done this exercise, it's time to determine what you think the Spirit is saying to you. How do you interpret, in the context of your own life, how these three Words from God are speaking to you right now. Consider everything on your heart.

As you go through this, relax and pay attention to the leading of the Spirit. Be prepared for the unexpected where the Father brings to mind a person, a situation, or event in your life that He wants to deal with. For example, unforgiveness (self and others), past unresolved hurt He wants to heal, a promise for your current situation, your family or someone in your family, such as your children. This is an exciting time where anything can happen (we even have experienced supernatural events such as a gust of wind dropping a bird's nest outside a sliding door that was a message for someone in the room) and is a chance to experience the beginning of a lifetime of hearing from the Father and experiencing the branch life. Understand that the Father is wanting to launch you into where He wishes to bring fruit (His fruit) into your life. He has much to say and promises to be clear in speaking to you.

As an example, a woman in one of our retreats was led to Ezekiel 34:16:

> [16] I will seek the lost, and I will bring back the strayed, and I will bind up the injured, and I will strengthen the weak, and the fat and the strong I will destroy.[a] I will feed them in justice. (**Ezekiel 34:16, ESV**)

This section cross-referenced to: Isaiah 40:11, which reads:

> [11] He will tend his flock like a shepherd;
> he will gather the lambs in his arms;
> he will carry them in his bosom,
> and gently lead those that are with young. (**Isaiah 40:11, ESV**)

This cross-referenced to: Psalm 23:1–6:

The Lord Is My Shepherd

A Psalm of David. 23

The Lord is my shepherd; I shall not want.

² He makes me lie down in green pastures.

He leads me beside still waters.[a]

³ He restores my soul.

He leads me in paths of righteousness[b]

for his name's sake.

⁴ Even though I walk through the valley of the shadow of death,[c]

I will fear no evil,

for you are with me;

your rod and your staff,

they comfort me.

⁵ You prepare a table before me

in the presence of my enemies;

you anoint my head with oil;

my cup overflows.

⁶ Surely[d] goodness and mercy[e] shall follow me

all the days of my life,

and I shall dwell[f] in the house of the Lord

forever.[g] **(Psalm 23:1-6, ESV)**

As we processed verses in the group, the woman openly shared that she had lived an inner life burdened by being broken and oppressed by the emotional abuse she endured as a child. She always felt condemned by others, self, and particularly God. (Because she knew this was mostly self-inflicted, she, over the years, had tried to overcome it on her own and even through therapy, but was never successful.) It was clear that she did not know God as a good shepherd who would carry her in love nor did she know any of the promises of Psalm 23. But, she found herself here with an invitation from God to be healed of this soul wound, and without which she could live a life of freedom. God offered her life through His Word and through His Spirit as she abided in HIM. We instructed her to write out Psalm 23 verse by verse. Afterwards, we encouraged her to cross reference each verse to other truths that spoke to her heart. We encouraged her to stay with this in dialogue, by processing and by spending time with the Lord (remember abiding in the Vine, not just Bible study) until she experienced real transformation and freedom, and was no longer living with these burdens. She did, and she is!

CONCLUSION

Now that you understand and have experienced hearing from God on a personal level, continue abiding in the Word that God has spoken to you a minimum of 20 minutes a day, every day. Continue to journal, and cross reference, always writing down what you are hearing, what questions and issues you have about this specific issue in your real-life circumstances, or how you are experiencing the truth of what HE is showing you and what you are understanding/discerning, etc. Stay with it! Do this day after day, step by step until you fully experience this beautiful promise that He has spoken to you.

Remember, He does not want you to just learn intellectually about this but to be transformed fully or to realize in the circumstances of your life the promise that He has given you. Do not move on to something else or only do a devotion each day. Instead, "camp" out, even if just 20 minutes a day, abiding with Him as you experience life with HIM. You will see Him working, begin experiencing peace, joy, and freedom along the way. It will feel truly remarkable as He fulfills what He has personally spoken to you.

Also, since you learned how wonderful and blessed it is to live in "Unity" (for there He commands blessing and because there you discover His will, which is best and none better) continue to practice seeking God's will together with your spouse or another trusted, Godly friend (if you are single) as you begin to seek God's will for all your decisions and issues of life. You will learn not to go to selfishness, debating, and arguing (division), but to enjoy processing together (even when you disagree, which is normal and good) until you reach unity and see clearly how to confirm God's will. Enjoy your adventure to the fullest!

CPSIA information can be obtained
at www.ICGtesting.com
Printed in the USA
LVHW071946080820
662709LV00052B/2101